THE SUFFOLK COMMITTEES
FOR SCANDALOUS MINISTERS
1644 – 1646

THE
SUFFOLK COMMITTEES
FOR
SCANDALOUS MINISTERS
1644-1646

Edited by
CLIVE HOLMES, M.A., Ph.D.

*Assistant Professor of English History
at Cornell University*

1970

SUFFOLK RECORDS SOCIETY

VOLUME XIII

The Suffolk Records Society was founded in 1958. The titles of its twelve previous volumes of records are:

1. *Suffolk Farming in the Nineteenth Century*, edited by Joan Thirsk, B.A., Ph.D., and Jean Imray, B.A.

2. *The Sibton Abbey Estates: Select Documents, 1325–1509*, edited by A. H. Denney, B.A.

3. *Suffolk and the Great Rebellion, 1640–1660*, edited by Alan Everitt, M.A., Ph.D.

4. *John Constable's Correspondence: I. The Family at East Bergholt, 1807–1837*, edited by R. B. Beckett, and published jointly with Her Majesty's Stationery Office.

5. *The Letter-book of William de Hoo, Sacrist of Bury St. Edmunds, 1280–1294*, edited by Antonia Gransden.

6. *John Constable's Correspondence: II. Early Friends and Maria Bicknell (Mrs. Constable)*, edited by R. B. Beckett.

7. *A Dictionary of Suffolk Arms*, compiled by Joan Corder, and with a Foreword by Sir Anthony Wagner, K.C.V.O., D.Litt., Garter King of Arms.

8. *John Constable's Correspondence: III. The Correspondence with C. R. Leslie, R.A.*, edited by R. B. Beckett.

9. *Poor Relief in Elizabethan Ipswich*, edited by John Webb, M.A., F.R.Hist.S.

10. *John Constable's Correspondence: IV. Patrons, Dealers and Fellow Artists*, edited by R. B. Beckett.

11. *John Constable's Correspondence: V. Various Friends, with Charles Boner and the Artist's Children*, edited by R. B. Beckett.

12. *John Constable's Correspondence: VI. The Fishers*, edited by R. B. Beckett, and with a Preface by Geoffrey Grigson.

The Society has produced one additional publication, *Great Tooley of Ipswich*, a biography of a sixteenth-century merchant by John Webb.

Published by the Suffolk Records Society, The Record Office, County Hall, Ipswich, and printed by W. S. Cowell Ltd, Butter Market, Ipswich, Suffolk

Contents

Preface

The publication of these documents concerning those ministers who fell into the clutches of the Suffolk Committees for Scandalous Ministers between 1644 and 1646 may be thought to require some defence. Since the appearance of A. G. Matthews' *Walker Revised* (Oxford, 1948), biographical notes on the sequestered Suffolk incumbents, and summaries of the charges against these clerics, largely extracted from the documents published here, have been available to scholars. My debt to Mr Matthews' work is large, and I have not felt obliged to repeat biographical information available in his book. It is in the latter that I find the justification for publishing these documents in full: 'the articles and the replies that have come down to us make good reading,' he wrote, 'and are but poorly represented by bare summaries' (p. xxv). In these documents the reader will find not only material relating to the reaction to national policies and decisions at a local level, but a good deal concerning rural life and culture in Suffolk in the early seventeenth century.

I should like to express my gratitude to the authorities of the British Museum, the Bodleian Library, the Lincoln City Library and the Ipswich and East Suffolk Record Office for permission to publish documents in their possession.

I would also like to thank the Master and Fellows of Christ's College, Cambridge, and the History Department of Cornell University, who provided generous grants for the microfilming of the Lincoln City Library Manuscript, and for the typing of the final draft of the transcription.

My chief debt is to the editor of the Suffolk Records Society, Mr Norman Scarfe; his encouragement, scholarly assistance on points of local detail, and patience, have been invaluable.

Clive Holmes

ABBREVIATIONS

Add.	Additional Manuscripts, British Museum.
Century	(John White) *The first century of scandalous, malignant priests*, 1643.
C.J.	*Commons' Journal.*
D.N.B.	*Dictionary of National Biography.*
Everitt	Alan Everitt, *Suffolk and the Great Rebellion 1640–1660.* Suffolk Records Society, Vol. III, Ipswich, 1960.
Firth and Rait	C. H. Firth and R. S. Rait (eds.), *Acts and Ordinances of the Interregnum 1642–1660* (3 volumes) 1911.
Harl.	Harleian Manuscripts, British Museum.
L.J.	*Lords' Journal.*
Matthews	A. G. Matthews, *Walker Revised.* Oxford, 1948.
Ms. Clarendon	The manuscript collection of Edward, Earl of Clarendon, Bodleian Library, Oxford.

Ms. J. Walker   The manuscript collection of the Rev. John Walker, Bodleian Library, Oxford.
S.P.   State Papers, Public Record Office.
Stowe   Stowe Manuscripts, British Museum.
Tanner   Tanner Manuscripts, Bodleian Library.
Walker   John Walker, *An Attempt towards recovering an Account of the Numbers and Sufferings of the Clergy.* 1714.

RULES OF TRANSCRIPTION

In the transcription of documents the original spelling has been retained, but for the convenience of readers, punctuation and obsolete symbols have been modernized, and abbreviations expanded. Doubtful readings and explanatory words have been italicized and enclosed in square brackets. Paraphrases to avoid the tedious repetition of the formalities in depositions are italicized, as are editorial notes.

Introduction

I. PARLIAMENT AND THE SCANDALOUS MINISTERS, 1640–1644

In a speech to the Commons shortly after the opening of the Long Parliament, Sir Simonds D'Ewes, M.P. for Sudbury, presented his ideal of ecclesiastical reform: 'It would be the greatest glory of his majesty's reign if we could change the greater part of the clergy from brazen, leaden – yea, and blockish – persons, to a golden and primitive condition, that their authority might be warranted by their godly example.'[1] In early 1641 such sentiments must have appeared realizable. The country at large was hostile to the Laudian church (an antipathy which gave added purchase to the traditional attacks on pluralist, non-resident, immoral or incompetent clergymen), and had elected a House of Commons sympathetic to demands for reform, and as yet undivided by the contentious issue as to whether such reform could be achieved only by a wholesale reorganization of the ecclesiastical system.

Three days after the opening of Parliament the Commons established a Committee of the Whole House 'for Religion', and immediately petitions flooded in from the localities, complaining not only of the obnoxious Laudian prelates and their aides, but also of individual incumbents.[2] In response to this pressure the House nominated a sub-committee 'for Preaching Ministers', charged with inquiring into the dearth of able preachers, with considering means of providing the latter with an adequate maintenance, and with investigating ways of removing 'Scandalous ministers' and replacing them with more satisfactory incumbents.[3] It was further suggested that all M.P.s, upon their own knowledge and upon information from their counties, should provide the Committee with an account of the state of the clergy in their shires within six weeks. A pirate edition of this order was published in which it was suggested that the Commons would welcome certificates from 'all ingenuous persons in every county' of benefices held by pluralists, non-preachers or 'persecuting, innovating, or scandalous ministers that they may be put out.'[4] The publisher was mildly rebuked by the House,[5] but it is clear that the pamphlet enjoyed a wide circulation – it was

---

[1] Quoted in W. A. Shaw, *A History of the English Church during the Civil Wars and under the Commonwealth 1640–1660.* (2 Vols., 1900.) I, p. 22.

[2] See the petition of Ipswich (Tanner 220 ff. 7–43).

[3] C. J., II, p. 54. In the Journals of the House of Commons this Committee is usually referred to as 'the Committee for Scandalous Ministers', although its original title is used occasionally.

[4] *An order made to a select committee chosen by the whole House of Commons to receive petitions touching ministers* (1640).

[5] C.J., II,.p. 65. See also (–Chestlin), *Persecutio Undecima* (1681), p. 10.

certainly available in Suffolk[1] – and the subsequent response to the institution of the Committee may in part be ascribed to it; Dr Shaw estimated that eight hundred petitions were presented to the Committee in the first few months of its existence.[2]

But the initial enthusiasm in Parliament produced nothing positive. As an increasing weight of business demanded the attention of M.P.s, certain Committees, whose investigations were considered of less immediate importance, were suppressed: on at least five occasions the Committee for Scandalous Ministers was discontinued, only to be revived, usually on the Commons' receipt of a petition against a particularly disreputable or 'popish' minister.[3] Further, the House never determined whether it was the Committee's function to hear every case brought before it, or to draft a Bill of general application against Scandalous Ministers.[4] The latter was clearly preferable, but although the Committee presented a first draft in June 1641, the Bill did not receive its third reading until April 1642.[5] This tardy progress was certainly due to the intermittent sitting of the Committee, and to the fact that on each occasion it was resurrected the House would forward yet another petition to it for investigation.[6] The Lords' discussions of the Bill were no swifter: not until January 1643 did it pass both Houses, and by this date the advent of the Civil War had made its provisions unworkable.[7]

Whilst the general Bill against Scandalous Ministers never reached fruition, the frequent and time-consuming investigations of the charges against individual incumbents by the Committee were equally abortive. Some ministers were summoned to Westminster as delinquents, and imprisoned for breach of privilege in speaking against Parliament in 1641 and early 1642.[8] But neither these men, nor vicious or 'popish' incumbents, could be deprived of their livings without the case being forwarded to the House of Lords for its consent. It is impossible to state how many ministers were voted unfit to perform their ministerial function by the Committee,[9]

[1] The Rev. John Rous of Santon Downham copied it into his diary: *The diary of John Rous,* ed. M. A. E. Green (1856), pp. 111–113. The most famous response to the published order is *A Certificate from Northamptonshire* (1641). For another county return, see *Proceedings principally in the County of Kent,* ed. L. B. Larking (1862), pp. 101–240.

[2] Shaw, *op. cit.,* II, p. 177. Note that petitions against ministers in Norwich diocese were often referred to the Committee investigating charges against Bishop Wren; see *The Journal of Sir Simonds D'Ewes from the beginning of the Long Parliament to the opening of the trial of the Earl of Strafford,* ed. W. Notestein (New Haven, 1921), pp. 195, 200–1, 207, 234, 248, 298, 385.

[3] C. J., II, pp. 66, 76, 162, 193, 225, 229–300, 353, 441.

[4] First suggested in March 1641: see C.J., II, p. 109; *D'Ewes,* ed. Notestein, *op. cit.,* p. 517.

[5] C.J., II, pp. 183–4, 491, 596.

[6] The Commons frequently ordered that the Committee should concern itself solely with the Bill – but as often reversed its decision by forwarding petitions for the Committee's investigation. See C.J., II, pp. 109, 121, 193, 208, 212, 225, 311.

[7] The Bill's history and major provisions are discussed by Shaw, *op. cit.,* II, p. 171.

[8] See, for example, C.J., II, pp. 71–2, 159, 176, 299, 427, 502. I know of no Suffolk cases.

[9] Richard Drake of Radwinter (Essex) was condemned in February 1641; his case was never reported to the Lords, and he continued to minister until 1643. H. Smith, *The Ecclesiastical History of Essex* (Colchester, n.d.), p.p. 180–8. See also L.J., V, pp. 585–7.

but only three cases were ever sent up to the Lords – and in none of these cases is there any indication that the latter took any action.[1]

Despite initial encouragement, local demands for the removal of 'persecuting, innovating or scandalous ministers' received a minimum of practical response from Parliament before the summer of 1642. However, with the King's withdrawal from London and the steady drift into war, the treatment of unacceptable incumbents entered a new phase. The number of breach-of-privilege cases increased substantially as Parliament summoned those ministers who had read Declarations published by the King, or who had denounced Parliament from their pulpits;[2] imprisonment was the usual penalty, but in a few cases the Houses proceeded to deprive the offender.[3] Other ministers of Royalist sympathies, particularly Londoners, rather than run the risks of imprisonment or personal violence often threatened by their pro-Parliamentary parishioners, deserted their cures to join the King. In those areas controlled by the Royalists a similar process occurred, and a number of incumbents of Puritan sympathies gravitated towards London. The latter, often indigent, were a cause of some concern to Parliament, but in December 1642 the Lords suggested a solution: those Royalist incumbents who had joined the King should be deprived of their livings, which should be served by ministers 'plundered' by the Royal Army.[4] The idea was seized upon by the Commons, who set up a Committee for 'Plundered Ministers', which was to supervise the mechanics of the transfer of minister and stipend.[5]

Initially the Committee, having received a charge against a minister, would hear the relevant witnesses and the accused's defence, and then report their recommendations to the House of Commons. If the latter was satisfied of the incumbent's guilt an Ordinance was introduced sequestering him from the living and nominating a replacement; this was then sent up to the Lords for their assent. The Lords refused to make the passage of the Ordinance a formality and inisted that they should re-examine the case,[6] and the tedious duplication involved probably led the Commons to adopt a new constitutional procedure: after June 1643 the lower house abandoned the method of sequestration by Ordinance of Parliament, replacing it by 'orders' for the sequestration of the offender passed on their own authority, without any intervention by the Lords; yet another example of the erosion of the rights of the upper house in this period. After October 1643 the Committee's responsibility to report its activities to the Commons, never strictly enforced, seems to have been totally forgotten.[7]

---

[1] C.J., II, pp. 139, 144, 148; L.J., V, p. 585.

[2] One Suffolk minister, Frederick Gibb of Hartest-cum-Boxted, was imprisoned for reading the Royal Proclamation against the raising of men (C.J., II, pp. 684, 794).

[3] *Ibid.*, p. 870; L.J.,V, pp. 248–9.

[4] *Ibid.*, p. 510.

[5] C.J., II, pp. 909, 913.

[6] L.J., VI, p. 12.

[7] These changes explain the dearth of records for this period. Cases decided before June appear in detail in the Journals of both Houses; from June until October certain of the

1643 not only saw the growth of the Committee for Plundered Ministers' freedom of independent action, but a widening of its power and responsibility. Very shortly after its inception, the Committee began to sequester and replace not only those ministers who had deserted their cures to join the King,[1] but also those who had spoken against Parliament or read royal Proclamations.[2] Invariably in these cases concluded by the Committee in the first half of 1643 'malignancy', whether expressed by flight to the royal army or by preaching in the parish, was the material ground for sequestration, but where a minister was also of scandalous life or a proponent of 'popish' doctrine or ritualism this too was mentioned in the order of sequestration.[3] Finally, in July 1643 the Commons empowered the Committee to receive informations against scandalous or 'popish' ministers, even though malignancy was not charged against them.[4] Also, whilst the Committee's area of responsibility was widened, the idea that its major function was to find livings for 'plundered' ministers was quietly dropped: some ministers were dismissed without any replacement being found, while many of the replacements were ex-curates, or lecturers, or fresh from university.[5]

Although the Committee for Plundered Ministers acted with vigour in 1643, even its chairman admitted that its influence was limited to the Home Counties.[6] The major reason for this geographical limitation was financial, 'many that would give evidence . . . are not able to travell to London, nor be at the charge of such a journey.'[7] In July 1643, in response to a complaint from the Isle of Ely that the safety of that strategically vital area was imperilled by the machinations of Royalist clergymen, the Commons voted that an Ordinance should be brought in with all speed, 'to enable all the Committees in the several Counties to sequester the livings of scandalous Ministers, and to put religions and learned men in their Places'. Neither the demand for expedition nor the specific recommendation was met; in September an attenuated version of the July suggestion passed the House, by which the County Committees were instructed to hear the evidence

[1] One of the first sequestrations issued on these grounds (3rd February) was against Edmund Hinde of Whepstead. See C.J., II, p. 949; L.J., V, p. 585; Harl. 164, ff., 286–286v.

[2] See, for example, L.J., V, pp. 632, 635.

[3] *Ibid.*, p. 715.

[4] C.J., III, p. 183.

[5] Walker, p. 73.

[6] See White's Introduction to the *Century*, sig. A2v.; 79·5 per cent of those cases recorded in the Journals of either House before October 1643 are from London, Kent, Surrey, Middlesex, Hertfordshire and Essex.

[7] Firth and Rait, I, p. 371.

Commons' orders are summarily reported in their Journal. Thereafter 'official' records are silent until January 1645. However, some cases not in the Journals are recorded in the *Century*, published in November 1643 by John White, chairman of the Committee. For example 4 Suffolk cases are recorded in the Journals, and 2 of these plus 16 other cases are in the *Century*. But it is clear that other Suffolk ministers were sequestered in 1643 whose cases appear in neither source.

against a minister, and to send the testimonies and the accused's answer to Westminster for final determination by the Plundered Ministers' Committee.[1] In late 1643 the Suffolk Committee[2] was operating in accordance with these instructions: Richard Davenport, vicar of Stowlangtoft, complained to Sir Simonds D'Ewes that the evidence against him had been dispatched to Westminster before his answer was prepared, through the malice of Sir William Spring of Pakenham, despite an order from the Suffolk Committee to the contrary.[3]

This system, whereby evidence was heard locally, but the case decided in London, remained in force for most of England until the end of the Civil War. However, in a series of Ordinances passed in 1644 a system similar to that proposed in July was introduced for certain counties, chiefly those where Royalist forces were still operating, whereby the evidence was heard and judgement passed either by a local Committee or commander.[4] The Earl of Manchester's Ordinance of the 22nd January 1644[5] was the first in this series, covered the largest region, and is the only example for an area where the danger from Royalist troops was negligible.

That Manchester was granted this unprecedented Ordinance is a measure of the support which he received from the most active groups in the House of Commons.[6] Although the prime purpose of the legislation was religious, in particular an attempt to reform Cambridge University,[7] financial considerations may also have been involved in its passage. In November 1643 Manchester came to Westminster from his military command to press for measures that would obviate those financial difficulties which had prevented him from capitalizing on his victories at Lynn and Winceby. Within a few days an Ordinance was introduced to tighten the financial administration of his army; it included a clause to enable him to sequester and replace scandalous ministers.[8] However, this legislation came to nothing, as did another attempt to introduce the scandalous ministers clause as a separate Ordinance in December.[9] The measure finally passed in January after the military leaders of the eastern counties' army had massed in London to ensure 'that for the future a constant pay may be had for them',[10]

[1] C.J., III, pp. 153, 231.

[2] The general administrative Committee of the County, whose Committee Book, 1641–1645, is published in Everitt, pp. 37–71.

[3] Harl. 387, f. 45.

[4] Cheshire; Gloucestershire; Shropshire ;Oxfordshire, Buckinghamshire and Berkshire; Wiltshire; Worcestershire. Firth and Rait, I, pp. 413, 431, 449, 457, 478, 510.

[5] *Ibid.*, pp. 371–2.

[6] For this point and the subsequent section, see my unpublished Ph.D. thesis, *The Eastern Association*, Cambridge 1969, chapter IV.

[7] In mid-1642 Sir Edmund Moundeford of Feltwell had seen the necessity of this: 'if these fountaines be not purged wee are like to have bitter streames the kingdome over.' Tanner 63, f. 116.

[8] C.J., III, pp. 307, 313; Add. 18779, ff. 5v–6; Harl. 165, f. 210v.

[9] Harl. 165, ff. 240v–241, 245.

[10] *The Parliament Scout*, No. 30, p. 253.

an aim realized in the financial and administrative provisions of the Ordinance of the 20th January.[1] Not only was the introduction of the legislation enabling Manchester to deal with scandalous ministers contemporary with an effort to improve the administrative-financial structure of his military machine, but in the local petitions with which the Earl backed his Parliamentary campaign the clauses desiring legislation against scandalous ministers stress their political influence: their anti-Parliamentary propaganda was reflected in the unwillingness of their parishes to contribute voluntarily, to pay taxes, to provide recruits.[2]

II. THE SUFFOLK COMMITTEES
FOR SCANDALOUS MINISTERS

(a) *Institution and personnel*

Between the 24th February and the 15th March 1644, Manchester, as empowered by the Ordinance, commissioned these new Committees to serve in the constituent counties of the Eastern Association, each man being paid 5/– a day for his services. With each commission the Earl also sent a set of nine Instructions for the guidance of his nominees, and a letter exhorting them to diligence: it now lay in their power to remedy those abuses under which 'the people of this Kingdome have formerly suffered in their persons, soules and estates.'[3]

The Earl issued commissions appointing two Committees for Suffolk, each of ten men in accordance with the terms of the Ordinance, on the 12th March.[4] Two Committees were also instituted in both Norfolk and Essex, and in all three cases the intention was to secure 'easines of access'; Manchester was determined that prosecutions should not be discouraged by the need for the complainants to travel any great distance to press their charges. In Essex the personnel of one Committee were drawn primarily from the north of the County, and the other from the south; in Suffolk the division is between the east and the west. To further ensure the accessibility of the local tribunals, Manchester suggested that they should be peripatetic. But although the Committee appointed for eastern Suffolk spent one day in session at 'The Griffen' at Yoxford, hearing five cases from the northeast of the county, all its other recorded meetings were held at Ipswich, while the western Committee met exclusively at Bury St. Edmunds. However, Manchester's intention was furthered by the fact that prosecutors were not

---

[1] Firth and Rait, I, pp. 368–371.

[2] Everitt, pp. 45–6.

[3] The commissions for all the seven counties, and the letter and instructions to the Lincolnshire Committee are transcribed by Sir Francis Hill, *The Royalist Clergy of Lincolnshire*, Lincolnshire Architectural and Archaeological Society Reports (New Series), Vol. II, pp. 119–121. On receipt of the three documents the Suffolk Committee entered them in their minute book: Everitt, pp. 62–4.

[4] The names of those commissioned, and their attendances at the recorded meetings of Committees are tabulated in the Appendix.

limited to making their complaints within their own County; so two cases from northern Suffolk were examined by the Norfolk Committee, in session at Diss.[1]

The subsequent history of the two Suffolk Committees for scandalous ministers was largely determined by the previous development of the Committee system in the County. Unlike Essex, where the central County Committee sitting at Chelmsford merely supervised the activities of various 'divisional' Committees, each administering a grouping of hundreds, the entire administration of Suffolk was centralised at Bury; as the County sequestrator wrote, 'we have deverse devisions in our County, ... but we have but one Committee sitting constantly at Bury, our Committee being devided into fower partes, one part sitting in every weeke.'[2] Consequently the western Committee became virtually a sub-Committee of the general County Committee sitting at Bury: Edmund Lelam doubled as clerk to both Committees, while it appears from the attendance lists of the eight recorded meetings of the scandalous ministers Committee for the western area, that every man mentioned in either of Manchester's commissions who was at Bury, presumably attending the general session of the County Committee, could be present at the examination of the charges against a minister.[3] The eastern Committee, by contrast, was a distinct entity. Attendance at Ipswich was solely for the purpose of examining a minister; it could not be combined with the performance of the general administrative tasks of a Committee-man. Accordingly, with one exception,[4] only those nominated to sit on the eastern Committee attended at Ipswich, and, moreover, vicinity to the town and lack of engagement in other administrative tasks determined the relative frequency of the attendance of Manchester's nominees. Wentworth and the Brewsters from the north-east of the County attended seldom, as did Nathaniel and Francis Bacon of Ipswich who were active in the central administration of the Association at Cambridge. In consequence the meetings of the eastern Committee were dominated by a caucus of five men from the Ipswich area, of low social status and no pre-Civil War administrative experience, at least two of whom, Fisher and Duncon, had been bitter opponents of Laudian innovation, and had been persecuted by Wren.[5] These were the men 'with neyther good bloud nor breeding in them' denounced by the Rev. George Carter.

---

[1] Why the case against Proctor of Stradishall was examined at Cambridge rather than by the Committee at Bury is inexplicable. It might be considered that the hearing before the 'Commissioners for scandalous Ministers sittinge at Cambridge for the seaven associated Countyes' was undertaken because of the gravity of the charges; but the Committeemen who examined the case were not, as their title suggests, the general Committee of the Association drawn from all the constituent counties, but consisted of civic worthies of Cambridge and Cambridgeshire gentry of no great social status.

[2] S.P. 28/255 unfoliated: 1644 9th July, John Base to the London Committee of Accounts. See also Ipswich and East Suffolk Record Office, EE 1/01/1, f. 87.

[3] See Appendix to Introduction.

[4] Thomas Tirrell of Gipping, whose house lay midway between Bury and Ipswich.

[5] S.P. 16/437/91; *D'Ewes* (ed. Notestein), *op. cit.*, p. 234.

(b) *Procedure*

The basic procedure to be followed by the local Committees was set out in Manchester's Instructions, although these were to be modified in practice. The Committees were to proceed against any minister or schoolmaster who was non-resident, incompetent or idle, scandalous either in life or doctrine, or in any way ill-affected to Parliament, and to that end were to encourage charges to be brought by parishioners. Further, since many villagers were unwilling to depose against the local incumbent, either because the latter had bribed them with favourable tithe demands, or because the parishioners were enemies to the Reformation desired by Parliament and were unwilling 'to come under a powerfull minestry', the Committee were to summon some 'well-affected' men from every Hundred who were to inform against scandalous ministers in their area. On receipt of a charge against a minister, the Committee were to issue warrants summoning the prosecution's witnesses, whose evidence was taken upon oath. The accused minister, who was not permitted to be present at the taking of the depositions for fear of his 'discountenancinge the witnesses', was given a copy of the sworn testimonies, and was to bring in his defence, in the form of an Answer to the Articles within fourteen days. Regrettably the Lincoln City Library Manuscript contains no copies of the accused ministers' Answers,[1] but it appears that two incumbents, Crofts and Parsons, did not exercise their right as they had joined the Royal Army, that Lindsell confessed the substantial truth of the Articles against him, and that Raymond, Utting, Sugden and Ferror, though allowed longer than the statutory fourteen days, failed to return an Answer. The absence of any note that the minister had failed to answer his accusers in the remaining cases suggests that they had exercised this right.[2]

These procedures, outlined in the Instructions, received some modification in practice. William Keeble of Ringshall pressed to be allowed not only to make an Answer to his accusers' Articles, but to present witnesses to substantiate his case. The Ipswich Committee refused the request as neither the Ordinance of the 22nd January nor the Instructions gave a minister this right, but, on petition, Manchester accepted the testimonies of Keeble's witnesses, adding a proviso that the plaintiffs might make a Replication to the Answer. Subsequently this became standard form; in three other cases Replications were made to the ministers' Answers, and in that of Beale of Ash Bocking it is clear that the accused had produced witnesses to substantiate his defence. In the case of George Carter of Elmsett and Whatfield Manchester allowed the minister's witnesses not only to testify to his excellent performance of his ministerial function, but to impeach the credit of the prosecution's witnesses. This, too, seems to have been common form; when, in August 1645, Reynolds of Wixoe informed the Westminster Committee that he had not been given any opportunity to produce witnesses to prove

---

[1] The one surviving Answer, preserved in the archives of the Borough of Aldeburgh, is printed below, pp. 117–19.

[2] There is positive evidence for this in six cases; in those of Beale, Walker, Rolinson and Keeble where Replications to the Answers survive; in that of Reynolds of Wixoe (Add. 15669, f. 138v); and in that of Playters of Uggeshall (see below, p. 79, note 1).

his defence or state certain legal exceptions to the witnesses against him, a re-trial was ordered.[1]

Having completed their examination of the case, the Committee were to forward the testimonies and Answer to Manchester's chaplains, Simeon Ashe and William Good. Should they and the Earl decide that the charges were proved, then Manchester issued two warrants, either to the constables and churchwardens of the parish, or to named parishioners, often those who had prosecuted the charge.[2] The first of the warrants ordered the ejection of the minister from his living, the second instructed the Earl's nominees to collect all the tithes and other profits appertaining to the cure, and to retain them until they should receive further instructions. If Manchester did eject the accused minister, then the parishioners were to choose a replacement. The minister they selected must have a testimonial from 'the best affected gentry and minestry' of the county concerning his fitness for the post, while the local Committee were to ensure that the nominee was 'very orthodox' in his theological opinions – no antinomians or anabaptists were to be preferred. On receipt of the petition from the parish and the testimonials Manchester sent the candidate to the Westminster Assembly of Divines who 'made trial of his guifts and abillities for the Ministry', and, if satisfied, issued a certificate to that effect.[3] On receipt of the latter Manchester appointed the minister to the vacant living, instructing those nominated to collect the tithes to pay them to the new incumbent; he might also order that a fifth of the annual income of the benefice be paid to the wife and children of the ejected minister.[4] In those cases, particularly where the living was of small value, when it proved impossible to find a replacement for the ejected minister immediately,[5] the sequestrators appointed in Manchester's warrant were to receive the profits of the living themselves, and were to hire a minister to serve the living each Sabbath and Fast Day. This system was hardly ideal. The sequestrators were tempted to fill their own purses from the profits of the livings,[6] or might hire ministers who had been ejected from other livings.[7]

Whilst the Earl's Instructions theoretically ensured uniformity among the

---

[1] Add. 15669, f. 138v, Add. 15670, ff. 24v, 48v.

[2] In 20 cases the warrant is not directed; of the remaining 15, 8 are to a group of parishioners, and 4 to the village officers. In 2 cases, Ravens of Chattisham and Beale of Ash Bocking, the warrant is addressed to the Committee for Scandalous Ministers, and in one, Barton of Grundisburgh, to a single member of the Committee resident in the parish. The reason for this divergence in practice is not clear.

[3] A selection of such warrants and testimonials is printed in Hill, *op. cit.*, pp. 121–7.

[4] A constant source of dispute between the new incumbent and his predecessor's family; in 1645 there were conflicts in 6 parishes mentioned in the Lincoln City Library Manuscript, which had to be resolved by the Westminster Committee (Add. 15669, ff. 114, 147v, 157, 184, 209v, 222v, 236).

[5] For example the livings of Hasketon and Hemingstone had not been filled three years after the ejection of their sequestered incumbents. Add. 15671, ff. 14v., 60v.

[6] See below, p. 79, note 1.

[7] This certainly occurred in Norfolk (see House of Lords Record Office: Main Papers, 1645, 'The petition of divers godly ministers in the county of Norfolk'), and may have been the case in Suffolk (see Ipswich and East Suffolk Record Office, EE I/P6/6).

B

County Committees, and severely circumscribed the latters' freedom of action, in fact there was considerable local initiative. Not only did routine practices differ from Committee to Committee,[1] but the east Suffolk Committee, without authority, could reject the first charge against Large of Charsfield without reference to Manchester, and, by placing its own interpretations on the Earl's warrants, could prejudice the case of Carter of Whatfield and Elmsett.

(c) *The termination of Manchester's commission*

From October 1644 Manchester's increasing distaste for the war, and consequent lethargic handling of his army, led to a breach with his previous supporters in the Commons. In February the latter pushed through the legislation for the national 'New Model' army, which involved the supersession of the semi-independent armies of the Associations, and the consequent abrogation of Manchester's commission as Major-General of the Eastern Association. No ruling was given on Manchester's position in relation to scandalous ministers, and a period of some confusion followed, most apparent in the letters of George Carter. By July 1645 all cases still awaiting Manchester's final decision had been turned over to the Westminster Committee, but it seems that some judgements reached by the Earl in the period February to July 1645 were subsequently challenged in London.[2] With the termination of Manchester's power, the procedure for the examination and removal of ministers reverted to that outlined in the order of September 1643, whereby the local Committee heard the evidence and forwarded a transcript, with the minister's reply to the Committee for Plundered Ministers for final determination. In west Suffolk the standing Committee for the County sitting at Bury was employed in the task of examination, but for the east the Committee for Scandalous Ministers originally nominated by Manchester continued to meet and undertake those local investigations required by the Committee of Plundered Ministers into 1646.

III. THE CHARGES

Accusations against ministers may be divided, for convenience, into three categories; the specifically religious, those charging the minister with being hostile to the Parliamentary cause, and, finally, those impugning his morals.

Excluding Watson of Woolpit and Goltey of Walton from the calculation, as the charges against both are concerned solely with their behaviour in their parishes after the sequestrations, 60·5 per cent of the accused ministers were charged with some form of immorality, 78·9 per cent with malignancy, and 91·7 per cent with subscribing to some obnoxious religious practice or

---

[1] Note the different form employed by the two Suffolk and the Norfolk Committees in taking testimonies.

[2] Despite Manchester's dismissal of the charge against Keeble on the 24th March, the latter's accusers subsequently resurrected the case before the Committee of Plundered Ministers: the Earl ejected Browne of Moulton on the 17th March 1645, but in September the Westminster Committee re-heard the case (Add. 15669, ff. 179v, 201v).

doctrine.[1] Indeed the only ministers not charged with offences in the latter category were Gibbons of Bealings, Raymond of Blyford and Utting of Corton, the accusations against all three of whom were concerned solely with their alleged gross immorality.

(a) *Religion*

Most of the charges in this category are concerned with the period prior to the sitting of the Long Parliament, although some ministers were accused of refusing to observe the Parliamentary Fast Days,[2] or of not permitting 'godly' ministers to preach from their pulpits, while a few were bold enough to continue practising the offending ceremonies 'even since the ordinance of Parliament forbidding the same.' Traditional Puritan complaints against pluralists, non-residents and 'dumb-dogs' – those who lacked the ability or inclination to preach regularly – are to be found in the charges, but the bulk of the latter are concerned with subscription to the ritualistic demands of the Laudians. The usual statement was that the minister was an observer 'of all the Innovations' introduced by Bishop Wren, Laud's determined associate in the diocese of Norwich, followed by a catalogue of those innovations: that the minister bowed to the east and at the name of Jesus, that he would not give the sacrament to any that refused to accept it kneeling at the altar rails, or that he insisted on performing certain parts of the ceremonies of marriage and churching women in the chancel. Nine ministers were accused not only of practising the ceremonies, but of prosecuting those parishioners who were not prepared to conform, particularly in the matter of the reception of the sacrament, in the local Ecclesiastical Courts. Charges of deviation from Calvinist doctrine were less frequent than those against 'popish' ritualism, although a few ministers were accused of preaching Arminian tenets concerning justification, of favouring auricular confession and prayers to saints, or of failing to demonstrate their hostility to the Church of Rome. One other aspect of the Laudian programme also figures in the charges. The *Book of Sports*, with its allowance of stipulated activities on the Lord's Day was utterly obnoxious to Puritan Sabbatarianism, and twelve ministers are accused of reading 'upon the Lord's day that Cursed booke of liberty for the prophaning of the same blessed day', and a further six are articled against for failing to rebuke those of their parishioners who practised archery, played football, or engaged in other rural pastimes on the Sabbath.

(b) *Malignancy*

Although two ministers, Crofts and Parsons, deserted their cures and joined the Royal Army, while a third, Watts, was alleged to have sent money to the King, most ministers were articled against for exercising their local influence against the Parliamentary cause rather than for actively supporting the Royalists. Six ministers, most notably Lionel Playters, denounced

---

[1] This figure excludes Gosnold of Bradfield and Bridgman, curate at Mildenhall, who were both appointed after 1640, and had not previously held cures in Suffolk.

[2] For these, see H. R. Trevor-Roper, *Religion, the Reformation and Social Change*, 1967, Chapter 6.

Parliament from their pulpits, while others refused to read the orders and justificatory propaganda emanating from Westminster, and four read documents of this sort sent from the King's quarters. The bad example given by clergymen who neglected to contribute to Parliamentary 'loans' or who refused to pay taxes until forced to do so by imprisonment, or distraint of goods, also appears in the charges. The accusations include not only a minister's public pronouncements or actions, but remarks drawn from his private conversation considered detrimental to the Parliamentary cause – his impugning the social status, religious principles and motives, or intellectual ability of the Parliamentary leaders, insulting Parliament's Scottish allies, or suggesting that the Earl of Strafford's trial was palpably unjust, and that the Earl of Newcastle was a good Protestant.[1]

While a minister's malignancy might be discerned by his accusers in a wide range of statements or actions, his reaction to three oaths – the 'Association', the 'Vow and Covenant' and the 'Solemn League and Covenant' – all expressing determination to maintain the Parliamentary cause, became a litmus test of his political sentiments. These three appear so frequently in the charges that they merit individual description.

i) The Association[2]

In December 1642, partly in response to local pressure, Parliament passed an Ordinance joining Essex, Hertfordshire, Cambridgeshire, Suffolk and Norfolk into a military alliance. However, the Parliamentary legislation was far more radical than that originally requested by the counties, and not until February, when rumours went round of a forthcoming assault by Prince Rupert to be backed by a rising of the indigenous papists, did local representatives, meeting at Bury, agree to implement the December Ordinance. In Suffolk the county M.P's came down into the country in March, and held a series of meetings to encourage the populace to support the Association,[3] while 'Books of Directions' were sent to all parishes. The books contained the 'Oath of Association', the subscribers to which promised 'to mayntayn and defend with our Lives, powers, and Estates, the peace of the counties, and to Ayd and Assist one another', and instructions for the raising of a voluntary contribution of equipment and money in the village to maintain a military force for the defence of the constituent counties.[4] The King, by a Proclamation, forbade his subjects to enter such associations,[5] and this may have enhanced the hostility of many ministers to the oath and the contribution, apparent in the Articles against them.

[1] Newcastle's forces, the most dangerous threat to the security of the Eastern Association in 1643, were invariably described as the 'popish army' in Parliamentary warrants and Ordinances, see Firth and Rait, I, pp. 291, 309.

[2] For a fuller account, see my thesis, op. cit., pp. 134-141.

[3] C.J., II, p. 956. For an amusing account of the first meeting at Ipswich, see the Royalist Diurnal Mercurius Aulicus, No. 9, p. 118.

[4] Returns of those who swore the oath, or who contributed, survive for Lavenham, Shimpling, Alpheton and Cockfield. Tanner 284, ff. 41-7.

[5] C.J., II, p. 998; III, p. 27.

ii) *The 'First Covenant'*

This is the Vow and Covenant, instituted by Parliamentary Ordinance on the 9th June 1643 in response to Waller's plot.[1] John Pym used the wave of horror which greeted the discovery of this attempt to betray London to the King with the help of a substantial fifth-column, to resuscitate a favourite, but previously abortive, scheme of his for a sworn agreement between all Parliament's supporters to defend their religion and liberties.[2] The Ordinance began with a preamble which referred to Waller's 'treacherous and horrid Design', and then invited 'all who are true-hearted and Lovers of their Country' to join together in a 'Sacred Vow and Covenant'. Those taking the Vow first declared their abhorrence of Waller's plot and their determination to prevent any similar design; then, moving from the specific to the general, swore never to assist the King's army as 'I do in my Conscience believe that the Forces raised by . . . Parliament are raised . . . for their just Defence, and for the Defence of the true Protestant Religion and Liberties of the Subject.'

The local implementation of the Vow and Covenant has not received much attention from historians, as it was quickly overshadowed in importance by the Solemn League and Covenant. However, as thirteen Suffolk ministers are accused of discouraging their parishioners from taking the Vow, and others with suggesting that the importance of Waller's plot had been grossly exaggerated for propaganda purposes, it appears that the Vow was imposed more generally in the localities than was previously suspected.

iii) *The Solemn League and Covenant*

The Solemn League and Covenant,[3] the Scots' price for their military intervention, was taken at Westminster on the 25th September 1643; on the 5th February 1644 it was imposed universally on all men over 18 years of age.[4]

Signatories of the Covenant agreed to use all their endeavours to maintain harmony between the two kingdoms, to prosecute all those malignants who had promoted the division of the King from his people, to defend 'the rights and privileges of the Parliament, and the liberties of the kingdoms and . . . the King's majesty's person and authority, in the preservation and defence of the true religion and liberties of the kingdoms', and, finally, never to desist from the prosecution of the war until these aims were attained. But the Scots were not content with a civil alliance; their assistance was motivated by religious considerations. The signatories also agreed to institute the fully-fledged Scottish Presbyterian system, and to extirpate not only popery, heresy, schism, superstition and profaneness, but also 'prelacy', defined as church government by Archbishops, Bishops, and the traditional administrative and judicial system of the English Church.

[1] Firth and Rait, I, pp. 175–6.
[2] See J. Hexter, *The Reign of King Pym*, Cambridge, Mass., 1941, pp. 28–31.
[3] See S. R. Gardiner, *The Constitutional Documents of the Puritan Revolution 1628–60*, Oxford, 1889, pp. 187–190.
[4] Firth and Rait, I, pp. 376–8.

The Ordinance of the 5th February imposing the Covenant universally also included precise instructions as to the manner in which the Oath should be administered. Copies were to be sent to the County Committees, who were to distribute one to every parish; the Committee should then tour the major towns in their county, where the ministers, churchwardens and constables of villages in the surrounding area were to gather, and, after an exhortation by a leading minister,[1] the Covenant was to be tendered to the assembled ministers and parochial officers. The Sunday following his taking of the Covenant, the minister, who had been instructed to read and explain the document to his parishioners as soon as he received it from the Committee, was to offer the Covenant to his congregation, who were to swear it in church and then sign a copy: the names of any who refused the Covenant were to be returned to the local Committee.

The Suffolk Articles give many examples of the ways in which a Minister, who found the sentiments of the Covenant obnoxious, might endeavour to circumvent the terms of the Ordinance: he might deliberately misinterpret its intention, fail to return the names of refusers, allow those to sign who had not sworn the Oath in Church, or add a clause declaring his adherence to the principles of the Covenant only in so far as they were compatible with oaths that he had previously taken.[2]

(c) *Immorality*

Of the twenty-three ministers whose moral character is impugned by their opponents, all but Sayer and Brown, who are only accused on the comparatively minor count of card-playing, are charged with tavern-haunting and drunkenness. Of these twenty-one, seven are also charged with being swearers, and four with being gamblers; another four are accused of being of 'indecent conversation' – which usually means that they had a predilection for bawdy tales – and five with either adultery or incontinence. While some charges are documented with an embarrassing wealth of circumstantial detail, in others they appear to have been added to 'round-off' a case against a minister. Walker's strictures should be borne in mind in regard to such testimonies; a peccadillo could be magnified into a heinous sin. That a man was a 'common swearer' might be proved by reference to a single 'by my faith', while 'tavern haunting', redolent with imputations of drunkenness, might be 'not other than the innocent Freedom of taking a Glass of Wine in a Publick House.'[3]

---

[1] John Brinsley, minister at Yarmouth, preached at the Beccles meeting: see his *The Saints Solemne Covenant with their God* (1644). A hostile account of such sermons in Suffolk is in Ms. Clarendon 31, ff. 29–31.

[2] Casuists suggested that such reservations did not necessarily have to be stated; they might be mental. See Tanner 62, f. 641 (1644, 20th March, Sancroft to Dillingham 'the Covenent is heere Universally taken, & our good people in Suffolk have soe perfectly learnt the mystery of *as farre as lawfully I may* that now nothing can come amise to them, were it Mohammed's Alfurcan.').

[3] Walker, p. 82.

IV EVALUATION

The charges of immorality raise the question of the reliability of the testimonies most acutely. The absence of the formal Answers of the accused
ministers does not assist evaluation, but in those cases where both Articles
and Answers have survived, as in Leicestershire, the historian is usually
confronted with two contradictory accounts, and has no means of assessing
the truth of either. Walker, following many contemporary statements,[1]
suggested that the charges were quite unworthy of credence, being presented by persons of low social status, motivated by malice.[2] There are
Suffolk cases in which a false charge was prosecuted to a sequestration by
the personal enemies of a minister; Whiting of Offton was reinstated two
years after his sequestration as 'it . . . . appeareth there was much malice in
the prosecution.'[3] Many of the charges in the Lincoln City Library Manuscript, such as those against Proctor of Stradishall for prosecuting his
parishioners for debt, suggest that the accusers may not have been motivated entirely by considerations of abstract justice. But though the motives
of the accusers may be questioned, this does not necessarily invalidate the
charges themselves. Even less convincing is Walker's denial of the veracity
of the hostile testimonies because the accusers were men of 'mean' social
status. Besides, in Suffolk the low social status of the prosecutors is not
universally the case. While the witnesses against the ministers of Bealings
and Corton, none of whom were of any great position in the parish, might
substantiate Walker's generalization, in most cases several local yeomen
testify against their incumbent, and in six parishes the list of witnesses is
headed by the wealthiest member of the community.[4]

Although Walker's wholesale denunciation of the credibility of the
Articles is not convincing, the historian should consider, with the Ipswich
Committee 'in this time of distractions how easy A thinge it is for men
abounding with mallice to finde witnesses to accuse men of our profession
to accomplish their owne endes.'[5] As we lack those insights into village
disputes and rivalries which might enable us to distinguish a malicious
prosecution, clearly no objective account of the state of the Suffolk clergy
could be based on these Articles alone.

But the accusations, used with caution, are not valueless. The Articles
provide some account of popular religious beliefs, and the penetration of,
and reaction to, the Laudian programme of the 1630s; they show how crucial
questions of allegiance were posed at the parish level, and how the national

---

[1] For example, Mrs Gilbert of Flixton claimed that her husband was ejected on the testimony
of those who owed him money (Ms. J. Walker, c. 1, f. 275). Also, see below, p. 106.

[2] Walker, pp. 64–6, 71.

[3] Add. 15669, ff. 89, 131; Add. 15670, ff. 20–1. See also the case of Rogerson of Monk Soham
(Ms. J. Walker, c. 4, ff. 397, 398).

[4] These conclusions are based on a survey of wills in the Ipswich and East Suffolk Record
Office, and *The Ship Money Returns of 1639–40 for the County of Suffolk*, ed. V. B.
Redstone, Ipswich, 1904, *passim*.

[5] See below, p. 118.

split might be mirrored in the microcosm of a Suffolk village. But perhaps most valuable are the splendid cameos of Suffolk rural life in the seventeenth century; of the constables of Blyford undertaking a midnight raid on an unlicensed alehouse to impress soldiers; of the Christmas celebrations at Little Cornard; of Nicholas Stoneham watching a Sunday football match at Eyke, to the horror of his Puritan parishioners.[1]

[1] The late R. W. Ketton-Cremer's book, *Norfolk in the Civil War*, 1969, includes chapters on 'Bishop Wren and his Clergy' and 'The Parish Clergy' which contain much interesting material for comparison with the experience of the Suffolk ministers.

Appendix

COMMITTEEMEN APPOINTED BY THE EARL OF MANCHESTER'S TWO COMMISSIONS OF THE 12TH MARCH, 1644

These two commissions are transcribed by Sir Francis Hill, op. cit., p. 120; that for East Suffolk is in Everitt, pp. 63–5.

The attendance lists are constructed from the names of the committeemen who, on a particular day, heard the evidence against a minister, and signed the written record. Eight separate meetings at Bury can be distinguished (1644, 16th and 20th March; 3rd and 25th May; 14th and 28th June; 14th November; 1645, 21st January) while a further 13 took place in East Suffolk, either at Yoxford or at Ipswich (1644, 29th March; 1st, 2nd, 15th, 16th, and 30th April; 13th May; 10th and 20th June; 2nd, 22nd and 23rd July; 5th August).

First Commission	Attendances at Bury	Attendances at Ipswich or Yoxford
Sir Edmund Bacon of Redgrave	0	0
Sir William Spring of Pakenham	4	0
Sir William Soame of Little Thurlow	1	0
Maurice Barrow Esq., of Barningham	2	0
Brampton Gurdon, snr., Esq., of Assington	3	0
Henry North, snr., Esq., of Laxfield	0	0
Thomas Tirrell, Esq., of Gipping	3	3
Edmund Harvey, Esq., of Wickham Skeith	3	0
Brampton Gurdon, jnr., Esq., of Assington	3	0
Alderman Samuel Moody of Bury	5	0

Second Commission	Attendances at Bury	Attendances at Ipswich or Yoxford
Sir John Wentworth of Somerleyton	0	0
Francis Bacon, Esq., of Ipswich	2	4
Nathaniel Bacon, Esq., Recorder of Ipswich	1 ⎫ 2	2
Nathaniel Bacon, Esq., of Friston*	2 ⎭	12
Francis Brewster, Esq., of Wrentham	2	4
William Bloys, Esq., of Grundisburgh	1	12
Robert Brewster, Esq., of Wrentham	3	3
Robert Duncon, gent., of Ipswich	1	10
Peter Fisher, gent., of Ipswich	0	13
John Base, gent., of Saxmundham	0	11

Not listed on either commission		
Thomas Chaplin, gent., of Bury	6	0

* The two Nathaniel Bacons create some difficulties in constructing these figures. In only three of the Ipswich or Yoxford cases do the original testimonies, attested by the Committee, survive; in each case the signatory is Nathaniel Bacon of

Friston. In ten cases both the evidence and the Committee signatures are transcripts, but in two of these cases the name 'Nathaniel Bacon' appears twice, so clearly both men were present at these meetings. This leaves 8 cases where the identification is uncertain. However, as Nathaniel Bacon of Ipswich was permanent chairman of the standing Committee of the Eastern Association, which met daily at Cambridge throughout 1644, and this position disenabled him from visiting Ipswich to perform his necessary duties as Recorder, it seems reasonable to assume that in all eight cases his namesake of Friston is meant. The case is less certain for the Bury meetings; only transcribed lists of signatures survive, but in one case the signatory is distinguished as 'of Friston', in another the name appears twice on the record. But in two cases it is not possible to distinguish between the men on internal evidence, and I have not credited the attendances to either man in the table.

On the death of Nathaniel Bacon of Friston in the summer of 1644 his place on the Committee was taken by another Ipswich man, John Brandling. (See below, p. 112.)

I. The Lincoln City Library Manuscript Book of Records of the Committees for Scandalous Ministers in Suffolk

A NOTE ON THE LINCOLN CITY LIBRARY MANUSCRIPT

The process whereby the Records of the Committees for Scandalous Ministers for Suffolk are now to be found in the Lincoln City Library is a fascinating example of a convoluted descent of a manuscript. In preparing his 'Impartial Collections' (1682–3) the Rev. John Nalson took from the Clerk of the Parliament's Office a large number of official papers which he never subsequently returned, and his finds included the Records of the Committees for Scandalous Ministers instituted by the Earl of Manchester for Cambridgeshire, Essex, Lincolnshire, Norfolk and Suffolk. How the Records came to be in the Office is uncertain, but it is possible that they were deposited with the Wesminster Committee by Manchester, after the termination of his commission, for use in any appeals against his sequestrations.[1] On Nalson's death (1686) his manuscript collection was inherited by his son-in-law, the Rev. Philip Williams, who seems to have placed little value on it – it was during his lifetime that Bishop Tanner removed a large number of the papers, which are now part of the Tanner Collection in the Bodleian Library. In this period the Records of the Committees came to the attention of John Walker, the historian of the 'Sufferings of the Clergy', but, regrettably, only in a very incomplete form. Charles Goodall, who conceived the idea of chronicling the persecution of the clergy during the Civil War independently of Walker, was lent the original Committee Books, except that for Norfolk which had been lost, and some epitomes of the books which Nalson had made; unfortunately, when Goodall abandoned his project and turned over the fruits of his research to Walker he gave him copies not of the original books but of the epitomes, which, as Walker realized, were woefully inadequate.[2] Goodall returned the originals to the Williams family, and they were part of the

---

[1] The absence of the formal answers of those ministers who availed themselves of this right, and the omission of certain cases where the Earl issued sequestrations – both Richard Topcliffe of Aldeburgh and Edmund Cartwright of Norton were sequestered by Manchester, but neither of these cases appears in the Lincoln City Manuscript – do not support this suggestion. (Matthews, pp. 330, 345–6.)

[2] Dr Tatham notes of these epitomes that they were 'apparently framed with the express intention of softening down the accusations with which several of the clergy were charged'. (G. B. Tatham, Dr John Walker and the Sufferings of the Clergy, Cambridge, 1911, p. 107.) The epitome of the Suffolk book is now in the Bodleian Library, Ms. J. Walker, c. 6, ff. 24–37.

collection in 1730 when it was rebound and rearranged by Philip Williams the younger. The descent then becomes more obscure. On the death of the younger Philip Williams (1749) the collection came to his wife, who remarried John Gordon, precentor of Lincoln Cathedral. Gordon's son, George, became Dean of Lincoln, and died in 1845. Some time in the century from the death of Williams to the death of Dean Gordon the bulk of Nalson's collection was deposited at Welbeck Abbey, although no account of the manner of its acquisition by the Duke of Portland has come to light. However, some volumes remained in the hands of the Gordon family, and on the death of the Dean in 1845 three volumes containing the minutes of the Westminster Committee for Plundered Ministers, and the book of the proceedings against Scandalous Ministers in Cambridgeshire were bought from his executors by the British Museum. Other volumes remained unnoticed at this time, and were kept by Dean Gordon's solicitors, the Carline family: in 1927 Col. W. A. Carline presented the Suffolk and the Lincolnshire books to the Lincoln City Library.[1]

Articles against Paul Gosnal, Rector of Bradfield St. Clare. Presented on the 17th November, 1643.[2]

I. That the said Mr. Paull Gosnall, about midsomer 1642, in one of his praires before sermon did use these expressions vizd. That the Lord would incouradge the King's Armies & Captaines & strengthen his soldiers, & that those which tooke upp Armes against them, their Armes might rott from their Sholders. (Robert Bragg, Thomas Worton, Laurence Hunt).

II. That in his Sermon oute of Jeremah 8 & the 7 verse at another time, he spaking of divers kinds of Birds, as the Owle cannot see in a cleare sunshine day, nor the Batts, but the Eagle is quick sighted, [said] yet now A company of Owles take uppon them to see clearer then the Princely Eagle. As wee conceive hee ment the King and Parlyament. (Robert Bragg, Laurence Hunt, William Rose).

III. Hee refuseth to publish in the Church any orders or Ordinances commanded to bee published by the howsis of Parlyament, but published the King's declaration concerninge the business at Hull. (Robert Bragg, William Rose).

IV. Hee is reported to bee a Common drunkard and haunter of Tavernes. (Robert Bragg, Laurence Hunt, Thomas Worton, Thomas Kinge, William Rose).

---

[1] This account is based upon Tatham, op. cit., pp. 92–6; F. H. Blackburne-Daniel's introduction to the edition of the Portland Papers (Historical Manuscripts Commission, XIIIth Report, pp. i-viii); and the introduction by Sir Francis Hill to his edition of the Lincolnshire book, *The Royalist Clergy in Lincolnshire*, Lincolnshire Architectural and Archaeological Society Reports (New Series), Vol. 2 (1938–9), pp. 34–43.

[2] These Articles must have been prepared for a hearing before the Westminster Committee for Plundered Ministers; it is probable that this body referred them to Manchester's local Committee on its institution. See the case of William Keeble of Ringshall, below, pp. 93–105. The first paper stands badly, without heading.

V. In one of his sermons about July he said they weare all Traitors that tooke up Armes against the Kinge, and said they pretended they did it for the safguard of his Person and the good of the Kingdome when they Assalted his person daly with fire and Sword & with great and small shott. And that they did mainetaine Theeves & Rogues & Whoremungers, and such as weare in danger of the law. And that they made Religion the cloake & stalkinge horse to leade them into all manner of Impieties. And that hee hard some Ministers wer Pursevanted[1] for speakinge against those men, but when hee should spare them he would that his Tongue would cleave to the Roofe of his mouth. (Robert Bragg, Laurence Hunt, Thomas Kinge, Thomas Worton, William Rose).

VI. In the same sermon, speakinge of Liers in Generall termes, [he] came to speake of state Liers such as wee have now, which bringe up Rumors of Forces which should come from denmarke, Spaine & France against England and that the Kinge should send for Irish Rebbells &c. And that the late Plott which should have beene in London are all arrant Lies of their owne Inventinge onely to scare poore men into Armes. (Robert Bragg, Laurence Hunt, Thomas Kinge, Thomas Worton, William Rose).

VII. Hee hath refused to Associate, absentinge himselfe Tenn or Twelve weeks together from his Cure about the same time; and for the most parte ever since neglectinge the daies of Publiq fasts, neither observinge the daies of thankesGiveing. (Robert Bragg, Laurence Hunt, Thomas Worton, Thomas Kinge, William Rose).

Gosnal is unmarried; the profits, tithes and parsonage house are let for £60 a year.

Taken before Nathaniel Bacon, Robert Brewster, Brampton Gurdon, Robert Duncon and Samuel Moody on the 20th. March 1643[2].

On the 22nd March Manchester issued a warrant for the ejection of Gosnal, and on the following day an order for the constables and churchwardens to collect the tithes and other benefits appertaining to the Rectory. Manchester also received a petition from the Suffolk County Committee, unfortunately undated, but presumably from this period, stating that Gosnal had been absent from the parish for 6 months and forwarding the request of the inhabitants of Bradfield that Samuel Crossman should be appointed to the living. In August 1644 Gosnal was in Oxford, where he preached before the Royalist 'Parliament' (P. Gosnold, A sermon preached . . . the ninth day of Aug. 1644. Oxford. 1644.)

Articles against John Watson, rector of Woolpit.

'The examinations of Divers of the Inhabitants of Woolpitt and other adiacent neighbours, taken before the Comitte at Bury St. Edmunds this eight daye of March 1643, agaynst John Watson, Clerke, Late Rector of the parish Church of Woolpitt, Frances Wells, Richard Walker and Hester [his]

[1] i.e. 'pursuivanted' – summoned to Westminster by an official messenger to answer their offences before the Commons.

[2] i.e. 20th March 1644; in the seventeenth century the new year began on the 25th March.

wife, Thomas Nice, Ambrosse Nice, James Hardy, Robert Clarke, Richard Crosse senior, & Edward Hurt, a trooper under Captayne Margerame,[1] according to the command of the Right Honourable the Earle of Manchester upon theire petition exhibited to him, as followeth:

I. This (John Houlder senior) examinyed saith that on tewsday the 27th of February, being the daye before the fast, John Miles with others of the Complainants did demaund the key of the Church doore of this examnate, to whome he delivered it & that then the Church doore was left lockt. And further saith that the next daye, beeing the fast day, Mr Frances Welles, being one of the Malignant partie, came to this examinat's house to demaund the key of the Church-doore, whereupon hee went with this examinate into the Churchyeard, & this examinate with another key opened the Church-Doore, whereupon Parson Watson with others came into the Church & read service and preached. And George Woodward saith that Walker with others went with Mr Watson to Church, and he saith that he heard the said Mr Walker say he would deffend Mr Watson from fourtie men. And Mr George How saith that he saw Welles & Walker assist Mr Watson to Church, and Walker did usher him to the deske the saboath day following.

II. Examined (Robert Parke, John Milles, William Sparrow, Phillipa Brett) saith that upon Tewsday the 27th of February they went to the house of Mr Watson aforesaid, & delivered him the sequestration; and when they were coming his wife said Heere comes your knaves. Then the said Parson Watson tooke the sequestration & read it and put it upp and would not let them have it any more.

III. Examined (Roger Barton, John Tebb, Peter Gooday, John Milles, George Woodward) saith that upon the fast day in the afternoone Richard Walker came into the Church with a woodknife by his side and a staffe in his hand & Francis Welles with a stafe in his hand, and theire attendance was Thomas Nice, Ambrose Nice, James Hardy, Robert Clarke & the wife of Richard Walker, whoe in a disordered way, all of them out of theire seats, reviled us the complainants in the Church, whereby they might provoke us to strike some of them. And Walker's Wife pulled Robert Park's hatt of his head and threw it downe at his feet to Provoke him.

IV. They (Richard Crewes, Roger Barton, John Milles, John Tebb, Peter Gooday, George Woodward) say that Parson Watson got into the deske and would not come out at our earnest request to give place to another Godly minister whome we had provided to preach, but continued gaurded with the

---

[1] Captain Ralph Margery. Margery's troop was raised in Suffolk, and was attached to Cromwell's regiment. The Captain was a yeoman of Walsham-le-Willows (Bury and West Suffolk Record Office E.L. 159/12/26-7), and this created some difficulties with the Committee of Suffolk, who objected to such a position being given to a man of low social status; their opposition provoked Cromwell's famous comment, 'I had rather have a plain russet-coated captain that knows what he fights for, and loves what he knows, than that which you call a gentleman and is nothing else'. However, it appears from the depositions that Hurt was scarcely one of those 'conscientious men' who, Cromwell assured the Suffolk Committee, would follow 'godly, honest' Captain Margery. (See W. C. Abbott, *The Writings and Speeches of Oliver Cromwell*, Vol. 1 (Cambridge, Mass., 1937), pp. 256, 261-2.)

aforenamed Malignants [*who*] did as much as in them lay by theire unruly tongues provoke us the Complainants as before. And the said Parson Watson said that the minister whome we had procured should not preach (which was in opposition of the ordinance of Parliament). And further they say that there came in one Edward Hurt, an unruly Trooper, with a pistoll & sword (by all probabillitie at the request of the aforenamed Mallignants, as did appeere unto us by their imbrasing & thringing[1] one to another) and demaunded of us the Complainants to shew our authoritie. Whereuppon We read to them all (with an audable voyce) a coppy of the sequestration and order. Then the said unruly Trooper, when he had heard it read, together with Richard Walker and Francis Wells, two of the Mallignants said it was a tale of a Cocke & bull & begane to revile us; and thereuppon Parson Watson & the rest of the Mallignants gave a farwell shout and Laughed us out of Countenance, and some of them said your knavery doeth now appeare. And the Trooper Hurt cocked his Pistoll & bad the Parson Watson goe one, and hee would see whoe dare oppose him.[2]

V. They (George Woodward, Robert Parke) say that after Parson Watson had done his devotion (for there was noe sermon that afternoone) Thomas & Ambrose Nice and James Hardy, to shew theire invetered Malice agaynst us the complainants, did pull up a stoole in the Church which did properly belong to Robert Parke, one of theis complainants, for to disgrace him. The Parson [*and*] other ill affected people [*looked*] on While they did pull it up.

Articles against Miles Goltey, Vicar of Walton with Felixstowe.[3]

I. That the said Miles Goltie said the Parliament was unconscionable in Sequestringe his said Viccaridge and proffitts. (James Cobham, Alice Cobbett).

II. That hee said notwithstandinge the sequestration hee was still Viccar

---

[1] Crowding together.

[2] In 1704 Walker received a letter from Francis Cocksedge, Rector of Woolpit 1678–1715, who had made some inquiries concerning Watson from his parishioners 'of greatest age and credit'. All testified to Watson's learning and exemplary life, and mentioned that his three prosecutors, named as Mills, Sparrow and Park, were unlucky in their business transactions ever after their prosecution of Watson. Cocksedge's informants also gave him a very different account of the Hurt incident which is worth quoting in full. 'The troopers comeing to town broke his house uppon him, and riffled it and took away the best of his goods and horse, and one Trooper, whose name was Hurt, a Mason, comeing into the Church the Sunday following put the good man into such a great fear and fright that he excused himselfe from preaching. . . . This bold trooper bid him read a chapter and pray as god enabled him, and he would set downe and hear him himselfe.' (Ms. J. Walker, c. 1, f. 302.)

[3] Goltey had been sequestered by the Westminster Committee of Plundered Ministers in 1643, and was one of the cases (Number 71) in White's *Century*. In the latter Goltey is charged with observing the Laudian ceremonial innovations, preaching against his parishioners going to other churches to hear sermons although he would preach only once each Sunday, and of dismissing a conscientious, preaching curate and replacing him with a drunken, scandalous, idle man. He was also accused of being a drunkard, and of expressing great malignancy against Parliament.

thereof, for that he hoped the times would soone turne, and therefore bid the Parishoners take heede what they did. (James Cobham, Robert Swett, William Glover, Alice Cobbett).

III. That being summoned to come up to the Parliament, he asked what hee should doe there, for there weare none but John anoaks & John a stiles. (James Cobham, Alice Cobbett, William Glover).

IV. That he said his name being in print he might lye in bedd while noone, butt what was in print was all lies and falce. And being asked who putt it in print, hee answered Mr White, but he had as good lett it alone. (James Cobham, Alice Cobbett, William Glover).

V. That hee wished the King and his Cavilyers were in Suffolk, [then] all wronges would bee righted. (Robert Swett, William Glover).

VI. That he said [of] Sir Ralph Hopton, my Lord Hopton that noble, that Valliant Commander, is gott into Sussex, and hoped hee would have the commande of it before longe. (Robert Swett).

VII. That when the first Covenant was taken hee would not take itt, for hee said it went against his Conscience. (Robert Swett, Thomas Segar).

VIII. That the said Miles Goltie hath endeavored to the utmost of his power, haveinge a greate faction in his late parish abovesaid, to devert them from adhearinge to the Parlyament. (Robert Swett).

IX. That hee, upon the 20th of January, beinge the Lord's day, he made a greate mutiny amost the Parishoners, in so much that there weare some blowes given. (James Cobham, Alice Cobbett, William Glover).

X. That he gave order to the Baliffe of the Hundred to warne many of the Parishioneers for their Rents and dues sequestered to the Hundred Court. And that the said Baliffe did on the same Lord's day [warn] them accordingly. (Thomas Segar).

That I (James Cobham, Alice Cobbett) can wittness that I hard the Baliffe say that Mr Goltie did give him order too warne them to the Court on the Lord's day.

Articles against William Alcock, Rector of Brettenham. These Articles were drawn up in February 1644, and were presented to the Committee on the 16th March.

I. The said William Allcocke hath beene a diligent observer of all Bishope Wren's Inovations, as bowing & reading towards the East.

II. He very readyly published in the Church upon the Lord's day that Cursed booke of liberty for the prophaning of the same blessed Day, which occasioned very much prophanesse in the parrish of Brettenham. Alsoe he very familliarly hath called our Loving brethen of Scotland Rebells openly in the congregation.

III. He hath expressed very much bitternes & malignancy against the Parliament & the proceedings thereof; his only companions are noted

Mallignants. He hath said they were noe better than traytors & Rebells that did lend plate & monyes to the Parliament.

IV. He hath often preached that Christians must not in [any] case resist the higher powers but obey them in whatsoever the comaund, be they what they wilbe, alleadging Romans 13, applying the same to the King.

V. That wheras some of his well affected Neighbours desired him to give them the soleme vow & covenant put forth the last Sommer by the Parliament, he, the said William Alcocke, replyed that he had taken the Oath of Supremacy & alledgiance & that he should breake them if he should take the Covenant, for, said he, this Covenant is directly against the King, and for ought that I know all those that take it are Damned.

VI. He hath used familliarly to rayle upon the Parliament, saying the Parliament is noe Parliament now the best of the Members are gone away from it, & that none are left but a few factious Fellowes; adding these words, [Parliaments] heretofore have bene for the good of the land, but this for the distruction of it.

VII. That hee scornfully demanded what successe wee had of all our fasting & prayers, & being told that God hath bene pleased to roote out many idle & prophane Ministers & planted zealous faithfull ones in their stead, hee Jeeringly replyed, I, but how long will they hold in. Alsoe being told that god had defeated many plotts, & the late plott as badd as the powder plott, hee presantly replyed, Who shall hinder a king from plotting in tymes of warre.

VIII. Hee sayd that when a man dyes his soule goes neither to heaven nor hell but abides in another place.

The Rectory is worth £80 a year; Alcock's personal estate is worth £16 a year, and his stock is valued at £60. He has a wife and three children.

Depositions:

to the First Article – *Laurence Raynham, William Makin, Ralph Wareing.*

to the Second Article – *John Durrant, Laurence Raynham, William Makin, Ralph Wareing, George Blomfield.*

to the Third Article – *George Blomfield, John Durrant, Thomas Bowle.*

to the Fourth Article – *Thomas Bowle, John Durrant.*

to the Fifth Article – *George Blomfield, Laurence Raynham, John Durrant, Robert Scott.*

to the Sixth Article – *Laurence Raynham, George Blomfield, Widow Elizabeth Hayward.*

to the Seventh Article – *John Durrant.*

to the Eighth Article – *Widow Elizabeth Fox.*

Proved before Nathaniel Bacon, Edmund Harvey, Brampton Gurdon junior, Samuel Moody and Thomas Chaplin, gent.

Manchester issued warrants for the ejection of Alcock on the 10th April 1644, addressing them to the Constables and Churchwardens.

Articles presented against Richard Watts, Vicar of Mildenhall, and against his Curate, Bridgman.[1]

I. That the sayd Mr Watts hath beeine vickar of the Milden hall this 12 yeares or there abouts, his Residence Beeinge at Chesterton in the County of Cambridge, 16 or 17 Myles a sunder. His Vickaridge at Mildenhall is worth £180 per Annum.

And, as wee are Informed, his vickaradge at Chesterton is worth £65 per Annum; his temperall Estate there £14 per Annum; an impropiation nere Coulchester worth £80 per Annum; his Lands in Ireland and Yorkeshire worth £500 or £600 per Annum. (Richard Parker, Hugh Waller, Robert Suckerman).

II. That the sayd Mr Watts did Contynew a Curate in Mildenhall afore sayd during his life, one Mr Blower, a man that did Preach Many Popish Doctrines and scandelos tenets in the sayd Church, viz: That he Could see noe hurt in the Crucifixe, but it was fitting every man shoold have one to put him in mynde of his Saviour. (Robert Peachy, Richard Parker, Hugh Waller).

That is was never merry world with Minestars since aurickular Confession Ceast. (Robert Craise, Richard Parker).

That conceyved praier was but vaine bablinge; that hee that made longe prayers was in a more dampnable Condition then hee that made shorte. (Spoken in the Pulpit.) (Richard Parker, Hugh Waller, Robert Craise).

That prayers are not soe needfull for our nessesarys as are the Churches' Commands. (Richard Parker, Hugh Waller).

That hee Read the booke of Sports for the Prophanation of the Sabbath openly in the Church (John Bird, Robert Suckerman).

That hee commented upon the King's Procklimation againstt the Scotts, Callinge them trators & Villans.

---

[1] These Articles are undated, as is the warrant ejecting both Watts and Bridgman from Mildenhall. However, Watts was ejected from Chesterton on the 12th April 1644, having been charged on 17 Articles, witnessed by 30 of his parishioners, before the Cambridgeshire Committee on the 19th March. As at Mildenhall, the Chesterton men stressed the wealth of this pluralist, but that, despite this, he was rapacious and grasping in his demands for tithes, and 'notwithstanding all this vaust estate he doth litle or noe good at all amongst us, neither in mayntayning the outward man or comforting the inward man; noe conforter of the sicke & little helpe to the pore'; they also suggested that he paid his curates very little – they were 'meanly clad both within & without'. Watts was also accused of being a promoter of all the Laudian ceremonial innovations, and of being hostile to the Parliamentary cause – neglecting the fasts, refusing to read Parliamentary orders, opposing the taking of the Covenant (see Articles VI and VIII below, which are verbatim from the Chesterton charge), and of sending two men, supposed to be papists, to join the King's army (Add. 15672, ff. 17v–18, 63). Manchester cannot have taken this last charge very seriously, for although Watts was ejected his personal estate was not sequestered. When the Essex sequestrators seized his impropriation at Elmstead for his 'malignancy' in March 1646, Watts procured a certificate from the Cambridge committee not only stating that his estate had never been sequestered, but that he had submitted to all the Ordinances of Parliament, paying all rates and taxes (Stowe 164, ff. 14v–15).

That the sayd Mr. Blower Preached againstt the Ordinance of Parlament, and was very Skandelos in his Life. (Robert Cattse, John Bailefe, Richard Parker, Hugh Waller, Robert Peachy).

III. That since his death Mr Watts hath set over us another Curate, one Mr Bridgman, a man very unable to discharge that place, as both himselfe & [the] sayd Mr Watts hath Confessed. (Hugh Waller).

That hee refused to publish the parlament's order, viz: for the Lord Farefax. (Hugh Waller, John Brierley, Robert Suckerman).

That hee denied to take the nationall Covenant and Endevered to hinder these deponents from takinge it sayinge unto them bee well advised & take heed what you doe, and that hee rather say that hee did not know whether it was Lawfull or not. (Samuel Flower, John Brierley).

That hee sayd to Mr Bright uppon a fast day Conceringe the sayd oath & Covenant that they shold never make him to take it while hee lived. (Edmund Bright).

That Thomas Marham Asked Mr. Bridgman where the Papists were; hee Answered are there not knaves in the Parlament's Side. (George Clark, Thomas Marham).

That hee disclaymeth the Cure or Care of our soules, and hath neglected (though hee was Requested by this deponant Sameuell Flower) to come to vissit a sick person, one of his Parishnors. (Stephen Pechey, Samuel Flower).

That hee speaked of frivelose things. Speakinge of weoman's Fundements in his Pulpit upon the text of the weoman that had the yssue of blude, he utterd such unbeseiminge words which made the Auditers ashamed to heare them. (Hugh Waller, Robert Suckerman).

That hee is A useuall Cumpany keeper of men ill Efected to the Parlament. (Richard Parker, Hugh Waller, Edmund Bright).

That the sayd Mr Bridgeman is a gamester & a man that hat beine diverus tymes disgised in drinke. (Richard Parker, Hugh Waller).

IV. That the sayd Mr Watts hath beine made Aquinted with the fore reicited misdemanors of his sayd Curates, And did putt of his sayd Parishnors with Large promises but noe performances soe that theire Expectations are deluded even to this day. (Richard Parker, Hugh Waller).

V. That the said Mr Watts & his Curate Blower have bene very Cerimonious, observing strictly Bishop Wren's orders (viz.) bowing towards the Alter, bowing at the name of Jesus, & praying for ArchBishops, Bishopps etc, causeing the comunion Table to be rayled about to there liking, reading the second service at the Railes both before & after Sermon where very few could here them – Mr Blower Churching of a Woeman there, & he the said Blower causing new marryed people to goe up to the rayles & at the end of the service there the said Mr Watts & Mr Blower pronounced the blessing at the rayles. (Richard Parker, Hugh Waller, Simon Suckerman, Robert Suckerman).

VI. That the said Mr Watts at Cesterton Omitted to reade that parte of the instructions that concerned the manner of taking the Covenant with his people in the said Church, soe that they are veryly of oppinion in case some souldiers had not come in the intrim & pressed & frighted him to it the said Mr Watts would not have taken it.

VII. That the said Mr Watts did pray for the Earle of Straford, giveing of him all his attributs & titles, after he was convicted of high treason by the Parliament, calling him his singular good Lord & Master.

VIII. That the said Mr Watts beinge commanded by the ordinance of Parliament to instruct the people for the taking of the Covenant, hee insisted upon the 14th chapter to the Romans & the third verse, inferring from hence this conclusion, that hee that tooke the Covenant should not iudge him that tooke it not and hee that tooke it not should not iudge him that tooke it, for wee must not iudge one another in thinges indifferent. (Sworne formerly by the inhabitants of Chesterton).

IX. That the said Mr Watts, before this Parliament began, came not amongst us above once or twice in the yeare. And when hee did preach the usuall subiect of his discourse & greatest part of his sermon was in commendinge his said parishoners for theire conformety to the orders of the Church. (Richard Parker, Robert Crannuse, Hugh Waller, Robert Suckerman).

X. That the said Mr Watts did not associate, never lent any money upon the Propositions, never subscribed any Armes nor would lend any thinge towardes the recrutinge of the Lord Fairefax or the assistance of our brethren the Scotts, although earnestly desired by Richard Parker & Hugh Waller. Nor hath done any Act, either by preachinge, discourse or example, whereby his people might bee stirred up to any conformetye with the Parliament, as these deponents know or have hard of. (Richard Parker, Hugh Waller, Robert Suckerman, John Brierley).
But on the contrarie hath encouraged such as are in actuall warre against the Parliament, giveing Mr Wentworth Bradbury the younger twentye shillinges to furnish him for his iourney, hee knowinge that hee was ridinge to the kinge's forces; and did write to a brother hee had then beinge att Yorke to supplie the said partye if hee were in want, & hee would see it repaid him againe. (Richard Parker, Robert Manbye. Mr Wentworth Bradbury the elder can testifie the same, but neglected to answer his summons).

XI. That the said Mr Watts upon a Lord's day since this Parliament begann did preach, administer the Sacrament, hasted afternoone service, sent for a Neighbour to hire his tithes, lett them, & ridd out of towne the same night. (Richard Parker, Hugh Waller, John Revell).

XII. That hee the said Mr Watts and his Curate have neglected to Catechise, wee havinge betweene 3 & 4000 soules in our said parishe. (Richard Parker, Robert Peachy, William Coe).

XIII. That Mr Blower, one of Mr Watts his Curatts did refuse to lett one Mr Dalton of Abbington[1] to preach in an afternoone upon a Sunday, although hee was requested to doe it by this deponent. (Hugh Waller).

[1] John Dalton, Vicar of Great Abington, 1633–43.

Articles against Thomas Tyllot, Rector of Depden.

I. That hee was a zealous promotour of Bishopp Wren his Articles and as a vigelent monitor did complaine of & endeavor to bring into trouble such of his neighboring Ministers as preached twice on a day, or upheld lectures. And that since the setting of the Parliament hee hath continued the ceremonious course of service, as crossing of Children in Baptisme, wearinge the surplisse, & bowinge to the alter.

II. That hee did read the booke of libertye authorising the prophanation of the Saboath, and, as a manifestation of his affection thereto, read it distinctly in the congregation two severall sundayes in the afternoone.

III. That hee hath within three yeares last past taught in his publique sermon that wee ought to direct our prayers mediatly by Saints & Angells to Christ and soe by him to God. And likewise defended the wearing of the Surplise, sayinge Ministers were as God's Angells and therefore ought to weare that white Garment betokeninge purety.

IV. That hee within lyke tyme hath taught that wee ought to obey the Churches' commands, lett them command what they will. (Thomas Fenn).

Although these Articles are undated, Manchester ejected Tyllot from Depden on the 15th April 1644. The warrant is addressed to the churchwardens and constables of Depden.

Articles against Samuel Lindsell, Rector of Stratford St. Mary

I. That the said Mr Lindsell hath bene a strict observer of the ceremonyes, as bowing of the name of Jesus, & in the pulpitt after the blessing pronounced, allwayes standing up at the Gloria patri, and constantly reads the first & second service, though hee hath oft bin desired to forbeare the same. (John Stephens, Edmund Anger, Simon Cooledge).

II. That the communion table was sett alter wise within the railes, which did occasion many of the parish to withdrawe themselves & not receive the Sacrament. (Simon Cooledge).

III. That the said Mr Lindsell refused to take the first protestation, & not onely soe but discouraged the people, saying hee, being our watchman, durst not but give us warning, wishing us to be well advised what wee did, & used many reasons to that purpose, which being there unto called, wee shalbe ready to prove. (Robert Barrett, Simon Cooledge).

IV. That hee the said Mr Lindsell hath never done any thing freely for the parliament, but constraynedly, & declareing himselfe thereby, as wee conceive, not to be of their mind. (Simon Cooledge, Robert Barrett).

V. That the said Mr Lindsell hath refused to take the last league & covenant, notwithstanding it hath bene tendered unto him according to the ordinance. (Daniel Wall, Edmund Cooke).

VI. That the said Mr Lindsell frequents noe lectures, but hath said that Mr Moore (meaneing him of Eastbergholt)[1] & such as hee is, hath bin the trumpett to blow up the warrs betweene the king & parliament. (Daniel Pickford).

1644 2 April. The same day Mr Lindsell appeared in person before us [*and*] confessed the articles to be true in the substance of them, whereupon wee forbore to examine the witnesses, & hath subscribed his hand in the presence of us: Nathaniel Bacon, William Bloys, Robert Brewster, Francis Brewster, Francis Bacon, Thomas Tirrell, Peter Fisher, Robert Duncon.

Manchester issued the warrant for the ejection of Lindsell on the 12th April, directing it to the constables and churchwardens.

Articles against John Crofts, Rector of Barnham St. Gregory, and St. Martin.[2]

I. That being in the Country at the beginninge of the Association and at that tyme being warned by the Constable to be at Stanton to associate [*he*] went presently away, and we never saw him since.

II. That when he did preach it was invectively against the Parliament, sayeing that he was greived in his heart to see them laugh in their sleeves in getting away their money under pretence of religious uses.

III. That att another tyme in his sermon he said the Parliament would soon be weary of sitting if men were not such fooles to part with their money.

IV. That att another tyme in his pulpitt he said if men would be such fooles as to be ruled by them (speaking of the Parliament) they would never leave till they gott all their money out of their purses.

V. That privately at the white hart in Bury he said he wondred that men would be such fooles to be so forward to part with their money for to maynteyne the wars, for if any were killed their blood would be required at their hands.

---

[1] Perhaps Richard Moore. In 1644 he was admitted as Rector of Diss, from which living he was deprived in 1662 for nonconformity. After his deprivation Moore settled in East Bergholt, which suggests that he may have had some previous connection with the place. (See A. G. Matthews, *Calamy Revised*, Oxford 1934, p. 353.)

[2] Besides being Rector of Barnham, Crofts was also Rector of West Stow, having been presented to both livings by his father, Sir Henry, of Saxham Hall, who had united the two Barnham livings by special licence from Charles I. The examination of the Barnham articles may have been perfunctory, in that Manchester had already ejected Crofts from West Stow on the 13th March, being informed of certain dangerous sermons he had preached there, and that he had been at Oxford the previous 6 months (the warrant is Ms. J. Walker, c. 6, f. 59v). Certainly Crofts was with the King in 1645; in August he wrote a letter to his father concerning the poor state of the Royal Army, which was intercepted and published (J. Crofts, *The Copy of a letter sent from the King's Army*, 1645). By 1647 Crofts had returned to Suffolk, and clearly had a substantial party of supporters in his old parish. In November John Legate, the 'intruded' minister of Barnham, complained to a Parliamentary Committee that not only had Crofts arrested him for detaining the tithes, but had forcibly seized the Church, while at harvest-time 'the violence of . . . Dr. Crofts and his Adharents' had forced Legate to 'garrison' his house with men hired in Norfolk. (S.P. 24/60 Legate *versus* Crofts.)

VI. That discoursing at Barneham about the Scotts with Mr Cooke (who wished they might come over to aid the Parliament) he said what the devill should wee do with the Scotts amongst us.

VII. That he was a strict observer of Bishopp Wren's orders, always boweinge at the name of Jesus, at his cominge into the Church boweing towards the Communion table, and so also when he went upp to officiate.

VIII. That the said Mr Crofts hath been absent from his cure twelve moneths & upward, and did not to their knowledge appoint any to supply the cure there; they say they have heard he is at Oxford.

Croft is a batchelor; the parsonage is worth £150 a year, but they cannot state the value of his personal estate.

Depositions taken at Bury on the 25th May 1644, before Sir William Spring, Maurice Barrow and Edmund Harvey Esqs., Alderman Samuel Moody and Thomas Chaplin gents.

Witnesses: to the truth of the
First Article; Robert Davy senior, aged 60, yeoman.
Second Article; Robert Day, Robert Gurnham, aged 50.
Third Article; John Buller, aged 35, Robert Davy, junior, aged 35.
Fourth Article; Robert Gurnham, Thomas Larling, aged 53.
Fifth Article: Thomas Davy, aged 60, William Hinsby, aged 48.
Sixth Article; Holofernes Cooke, aged 44.
Seventh Article; Holofernes Cooke, Robert Davy, Thomas Davy, Robert Gurnham.
Eighth Article; Holofernes Cooke, Robert Davy, William Hinsby, Robert Gurnham.

Manchester issued the warrant for Croft's ejection on the 8th July, directing it to Robert Davy snr, Robert Davy 'medius', William Hinsby and Thomas Davy.

Articles against Jeremiah Ravens, Vicar of Chattisham and Rector of Great Blakenham.

I. That the said Mr Ravens hath pluralitye of livings, and makes his aboad at Blakenham afforesaid whereby his cure at Chattisham is, for his part, altogeither neglected. (Daniel Meadows, Richard Fleck).

II. That he is erronious in his doctrine, preachinge Arminianisime; sayeing that man hath freewill to be saved if he will, and that all shalbe saved that are babtized, and that all being babtized are the children of God, and that a man may be the child of god today & the child of the Devill tomorrow. (Daniel Meadows, Richard Fleck).

III. That the said Mr Ravens is a superstitious observer of holy dayes, affirminge that holy dayes are to be observed before sundayes, and that his parishioners might follow their callings upon a sonday aswell as on a worke day, and thereupon did instance that a weaver might weave or any go to markett & buy & sell that day. (John Clerke).

IV. That the said Mr Ravens is an observer & maynteyner of Innovations. A constant bower at the name of Jesus; compellinge his parishioners to come up to the rayles in the Chancell to receyve the sacrament, refusing those that did not; readinge the second service at the Comunion table with much bowinge to the same service & table; and did use to elevate the cupp & bowe unto the same; also teaching and provokinge the people in service tyme to duck downe & make leggs & the woemen to curtsye, sueinge a widow woman in the Comissarye's Court for not sittinge constantly with her face towards the East in which said suit she expended betweene £30 & £40. (John Sexton, James Batle, Daniel Meadows, Richard Fleck).

V. That he affirmed if any will keepe a Sabath day he must keepe it on Saturday. (John Clerke).

VI. That he many tymes preached in the pulpitt sayeinge whosoever did not come upp to the rayles and submit to the Innovations & Bishopp Wren's orders should be damned. (John Sexton, James Batle).

VII. That the said Mr Ravens sued in the high Comission Court one of the Churchwardens of Chattisham afforesaid for removinge the Comunion table out of the Chancell into the body of the Church, and therein made him spend £36. Also sueinge others in the Commissarye's Court for goeinge to other Churches on the Lord's day when there was no sermon at their owne Church. One also he sued for puttinge on his hatt when he was gon out of the Church and steppinge into the porch. Others left their dwellings by reason of the said Mr Ravens his contention. (Daniel Meadows, Richard Fleck, John Clerke).

VIII. That the said Mr Ravens, to show his zeale for the bringing in of Innovations, did, contrary to his parishioners' knowledge & consent, sett men to worke to make & sett upp rayles, rayse the ground in the Chancell three stepps high, paint the Church, [and] bought a hood & surplice, to the overchanginge of the parish. (Daniel Meadow, Richard Fleck, John Clerke).

IX. That the said Mr Ravens hath been often seene very drunke and is a comon alehowsehaunter with such other preists as himself. And for the same, and the synne of adulterye, hath beene presented at the Commissarye's Court for the wife. (Richard Fleck, Edward Oxburrough, Robert Aldus, Samuel Duncon, John Clerke).

X. That he liveth most parte from his wife and maketh his abode at Blakenham, and, as his wife saith, keepeth a whore, one Cole's wife, and that it was well knowne to many there, refusinge his wife's company for almost theis two yeers. And hath hunge his wife upp by the heeles, and hath tyed his wife to the bedpost and whipped her. (Richard Fleck, Daniel Meadows, Samuel Duncon, affirme this from his wife's mouth).

XI. That the said Mr Ravens is a papist or else very popishly affected, as may appeare by a Crucifix and severall popish pictures hunge upp in his house; and being reproved for the same he answered they were sett upp to adorne & sett out his house. (Richard Fleck, Daniel Meadows, John Sexton).

XII. That the said Mr Ravens is a man very much disaffected to this present Parliament, for he hath not associated, and when the Constable of Blakenham went to him to know what he would lend to the Parliament upon the propositions he not only refused to lend any some, but said further in a most disdaynefull manner that it was a great sinne to lend the Parliament any some of money, or to do any thinge elce for them. It is also putt up against him that he hath suffered the houses to fall downe, therefore wee humbly desire that somethinge may be allowed for repayringe of them. (Francis Burroughes, the Constable).

April 2nd 1644 these articles were proved before Francis Bacon, Robert Brewster, William Bloys, Francis Brewster, Peter Fisher, Robert Duncon.

Ravens was ejected from the living on the 30th July by the warrant of the Earl of Manchester, which was directed to the Suffolk Committees for Scandalous Ministers.

Articles against Theodore Beale, Vicar of Ash Bocking.

I. The said Theodore Beale said that the Earle of Strafford dyed uniustly. (Thomas Bonham Esq., John Bacon, Matthew Birch).

II. That the Kinge was therein compelled by the Parliament & Parliament by the Rout. (Matthew Birch).

III. That hee would not administer the sacrament out of the Chancell for half his owne livinge. (John Bacon, Matthew Birch).

IV. That Mr Beale sayd there could be no comfortable conclusions expected from the Parliament no more then from the devill himselfe. (Thomas Bonham, Matthew Birch).

V. That the first letter of the religion intended to bee sett up by the Parliament was written in bloud. (Matthew Birch).

VI. That the lendinge of moneys to the Parliament could be no good intent, and if it had been to a good intent he would have sold all his bookes but he would have had mony for them. (Matthew Birch).

VII. That it was an accursed thing to take upp armes against the king's Army, and all one as if against his person. (Thomas Bonham, Matthew Birch).

VIII. That the greatest professors & hearers of the word had caused all this bloodshedd. (John Bacon, Matthew Birch).

IX. That theis great & diligent Sermonizers had sett God & the kinge togeither by the eares now at this tyme. (Matthew Birch).

X. That the two houses were full of Anabaptists, naming the Lord Say & Sir Nathaniel Barnardiston; and that the Anabaptists & Brownists in the houses were the contrivers of this present warr. (Thomas Bonham, John Bacon).

XI. That the said Theodore Beale hath been a Solemne Cringer & bower toward the East end of the Chancell & toward the Communion table. (Thomas Bonham, John Bacon, Matthew Birch).

XII. He at first denyed the sacrament unto such as would not come to the rayle, but after some tyme came out to them sayeing that instead of a blessing he brought a curse to them. (Thomas Bonham, John Bacon, Matthew Birch).

XIII. He hath refused to appeare to lend mony to the Parliament, and once, havinge left the Comissioners at Needham, repayred thence to Coddenham and thence tarryed drinking till 8 of the clocke at night. (John Bacon, Matthew Birch).

XIV. That he hath been many times disguised with drinke. (John and Thomas Bacon).

XV. He useth ordinarily to fall into invectives against the Parliament, & bestoweth litle tyme in other good studyes, and preacheth but once in a day. (John Bacon, Matthew Birch).

The exceptions against Theodore Beale, Clerke, his manner of administringe the nationall convenant to the parish of Ash Bockinge in Suffolk:

I. Wee are certenly informed that the vicar Mr Beale being then at Ipswich & present at the exhortation sermon, did notwithstandinge refuse to appeare to take the covenant before the Committee then & there appointed for the administration of the same. And they appeale to the role for the same. (Edward Turner, William Alderton).

II. The said Mr Beale, when he ministred the covenant to his parish, in his exhortation to the people onely insisted upon the common placs of charity and forsakinge of popery and draweinge neere to the best reformed churches; but used no reasons for the deposition of Episcopacy (in which many would gladly have been satisfied) nor for approximation particulerly to the Church of Scotland, nor yett incouragement of the people to resist the rebellion of the Cavaliers against the Kinge and Parliament. (Thomas Bonham, Thomas Grymwade, Edward Turner, John Bacon, Matthew Birch).

III. The said Mr. Beale called not to the people to hold upp their right hands, but without any solempnity, zeale or strict manner as was imposed & appointed, he onely underwritt the scedule, and in great hast admitted the rest so to do, as it were very confusedly. (Thomas Grymwade, John Bacon, Thomas Bonham, Matthew Birch, Edward Turner).

Articles concerning Beale's activities when he was Curate of Boxford.

I. He was a comon alehousehaunter & frequenter of pitcheringe or clubbinge houses. (William Parsons, Panrius Ellet, Thomas Bacon).

II. He counselled the said Thomas Cooper to putt away his wife because she made conscience of cominge upp to the rayle to be Churched, & counselled the said Cooper to keepe a maid & give her five pounds. (Thomas Cooper).

III. He hath excomunicated or procured excommunication against sondry good women for not coming up to the rayles to be churched, makinge some runn away from their familyes for two yeeres togeither. Others he hath so terrified that they have fallen into convulsions through extreme feare, breathinge threatinings & revenge in that cause so farr that he hath said he would not spare in that buisines his owne mother. (Thomas and Sara Bacon, Elizabeth Cooper, Goodwife Vincent, Thomas Cooper).

IV. Once in the pulpitt he used this argument (vizt) that Christ must save the greatest parte of people, otherwise he can be no Saviour, and that by the rule of Logicke. For if two Captaynes go into the feild to fight he that loseth the greatest parte of men, how cann he be said to be a Saviour? (William Crabb).

V. The said Mr Beale once procured an Excomunication against Goodman Watson & his wife, an aged man & his wife, for not cominge to service; who so continued excomunicated six yeeres at the least. (Widow Elizabeth Watson).

VI. The said Mr Beale once being at the deponent's house, being towards night, he said it was to late to go home, and if he staid all night he must lye with the yongest, she havinge her yongest daughter then present, a handsome yonge woeman about 18 yeeres of age. After this the said Beale procured this deponent to be cited to the Ecclesiasticall Court to prove her husband's will (which was to be proved in the prerogative Court), whereupon on Easter day next after she was excommunicated. Whereuppon she was afterwards arrested by five bayliffes & put to extreme trouble & charges, & forced to live out of the Diocesse ever since. (Widow Watson).

On the 1st April 1644 these Articles were proved before Thomas Tirrell, Peter Fisher, Nathaniel Bacon, William Bloys, John Base.

A Replication to the answers of Theodore Beale, Clerke, to certen Articles preferred against him by the Inhabitants of Ash Bocking.

Generally the answers conteyne an Appeale to the rest of the parish, or elce a recharge of the witnesses, to whom the vicar layeth malice & periury. For the first, which is an appeale to the parish, the witnesses reply that many of them are wilfully, and many ignorantly blinde; of the first sort they could name two, of the second sort too many, of whom enquire within one halfe houre after whether the vicar preached this or that doctrine, they cannott tell, they have forgotten. Wherein is to be seene brightly the Councell of Lysander the Spartan Kinge, what efficacy & influence the corrupted Oracles have over the minds of the giddy people. But we love our neighbours, and are well assured of them if prevarication were once banished the pulpitt, and some good light sett before them – which God for his goodnes send us & deliver us from the doctryne of all Imposters.

The recrimination principally reacheth to three witnesses, Thomas Bonham, Mathew Birch & John Bacon, who iointly answer that they expected no other then imputation of malice & falsehood, they knew it was the comon answer of all. But, say they, it were an unwise malice to take the Parson's bread of his table & deprive ourselves of the bread of life. Admitt, say they, there were cause of malice towards him (which they know none), why they should malice their owne soules they are sure they know none. Noe, the memory of their protestation & covenant, and the publiq cause sadly & severely propensed, and the notice taken how entire & whole congregations depend upon their Clergy, whether good or badd, theis are those things that stirred them upp first against the vicar and make them still earnestly wish for some good light to be putt into his candlesticke, that the pulpitt may no more be made a stage of witty invectives nor a Court for selfe pleas, nor bad example, a stumblinge blocke to their lives. But that there may be such doctrine & president as may lead the way with stronge assurance unto that blessed eternity whereof the mercy of God (wee hope) hath made us members. Thus much they reply iointly & in generall: particularly Thomas Bonham answereth for himself thus:

That he can make it appeare that in the whole processe he is free from malice, which donn & cleered the Parson must find some other ground for so gross a periury.

First, when the Articles were in frameinge he being required what he could bring against the vicar, answered that since his familiarity broke of with Mr Beale he had observed nothinge worthy of articling but that he said the houses were full of Anabaptists and brownists (witnesses, Matthew Birch, Edmund Mayhew.). And being further pressed to some particulars, answered agayn that he held it not Gentile to discover things formerly passed in freindshipp; and at the length, being strongly pressed with the protestation, & the dutyes otherwise of all good men to the publiq, he resolved, not without much striffe in himselfe to discover upon oath if compelled and not otherwise. Which resolution he kept to the end, refusinge to appeare before the Committee unles warned by processe from authority.

Secondly, after the Articles [were] framed, before exhibiting, the said Bonham of his owne accord did motion a peace, & treated upon the suppression of the Articles (wavinge all private iniuryes or elce reposinge in the lawes of the land for vindication of them), provided the Parson would promise a new life, preach twice on the Saboath & fast dayes, instruct & catechize the youth & become one of us for Kinge & Parliament. Yea, & had effected it likewise had the rest thought him a man capable of cure or recovery. (Witnesses, Thomas Grymwood, John Bacon, Matthew Birch.)

Thirdly, att the tyme of the exhibition of those Articles the Boxford people cominge in against him with matter very shamefull & unworthy his reverend Coate (whether strucken with memory of former acquaintance or for common humainitye's sake he well knowes not), he said there was enough already; nothing needed to be invented or inlarged. And, Christian-like, exhorted them with theis very words, Good people, rather speake a myle on this side then one inch beyond the truth or your owne knowledge. And this likewise was testified by three of the Boxford women (one Rolfe challenginge Bonham of malice on the Parson's behalfe), att that tyme before the worshipfull Committee. (Witnesses; Thomas Grymwood, John Bacon, Thomas & Sara Bacon, Elizabeth Cooper, Mary Vincent, William Crabbe.)

Now to the particular answers:

To the answer to the first & second Articles, Thomas Bonham replyeth that he heard not Mr Beale when he told Birch so concerninge the Earle's death. But that at other tymes he hath heard him fall often, & once in the hearing of Thomas Grymwood of the same parish; and protesteth that, not content to declare his owne single iudgement, he disputed the possibility of Justice in the Case, to that end, as he thinketh, to traduce the said Bonham to his owne scandalous opinion. Matthew Birch likewise denieth that William Alderton was by when he spoke to him of the Earle's death, & excepteth against the said Alderton.

4) To the 4th Thomas Bonham affirmeth this Article to be true as concerninge, "no comfortable conclusions to be expected"; indeed those last words "noe more then from the devill", he did not heare for he was not present when the vicar told Birch soe. But Birch alleadgeth the whole article at length, and challengeth Mr Duncon & Mr Caly of Ipswich, and Edmund Mayhew of Gosbecke to speake whether he informed them not of this passage & gave it them under his handwritinge about a yeare & an half agoe, longe before he was acquainted with Mr Bonham. And protested that he would informe against him although alone, and was terrified somewhat in conscience that he had not donn it already because of his oath of protestation.

5) To the fifth Mathew Birch likewise affirmeth the truth of this Article, and challengeth the afforesaid for his Compurgators. Therefore he humbly conceiveth that Mr Beale hath lighted on a very witty devise to iniure & wronge Mr Bonham by withhouldinge the truth in testimony at the law in a case betwixt him & one Rolph, theirby to raise enmity between them, and now to make use of that as a ground of Mr Bonham's malice and of all his accusers. But the tymes & moments considered it will appeare but a shift & no momment for the Parson in this case. He the rather conceiveth this because the Parson can (exceptinge this) not so much as pretend any ground at all for malice.

6) To the 6th Mathew Birch affirmeth also the truth of this Article.

7) To the 7th the deposers of this Article do offer further testimony (Thomas Grymwade.).

8, 9) To the 8th & 9th the deponents affirme those Articles as true & will affirme it to the death.

10) To the 10th the deponents affirme this likewise, and doubt not to make further prooff of it. (Oliver Thorne had process left at his house but appeared not.)

11) To the 11th the deposers wonder not at his stout deniall of this Article, well knowing the boldnes & wilynes of the answerer, and they suppose some mentall reservation in that mann. They wish he would remember his action & cariage in his goeing up to the second service: the deponent Bonham remembreth what Mr Aldhouse of Ash was wont to say (though he now expecteth he should forgett or deny it), that Mr Beale did indeed bow prettily & decently, as if he went to begin a dance, but that Parson Bucke of Stradbrooke (where part of Mr Aldhowse his liveing lyes) went to it like an

Idolater with three Congyes downe to the very ground betwixt his pue & the alter.[1] But he with the rest of the deponents hopeth it shalbe further made to appeare the truth of this article. For his appeale to his other neighbours, they have spoken their opinion in the preface.

12) To the twelveth the deponent Bonham confesseth that the vicar after long deniall, at the length came down and gave the sacrament to those refusinge Comunicants, for which the same day Bonham thanked and commended him for his christian humility; unto which the Parson then replyed, that he expected a letter from Bishopp Wrens, which had he receyved they should have come to the rayle, and this this deponent's wife can witnesse upon oath. Now why the letter from Doctor Wren should be to him such a directory the said deponent did much wonder, but that in the revolvinge of his thoughts he finds that the Parson hath often told him of a second livinge which that Bishopp had promised to add to this of Ash-Bocking, whence he gathereth that this Beale is a feather of his winge. And now not a litle is that coniecture confirmed since he hath lately betaken him to the Chauntry at Spraughton, the house belonginge to the said Bishopp's wife's father, as is informed. But the rest of the deponents to this Article do instance in another tyme after this (when Mr Bonham was not present) in which he would not budge from the rayle (by this tyme belike he had received the letter), by meanes whereof foure Comunicants at the least for their meere tendernes of conscience were driven from that blessed feast. And at that tyme there was a painted Crucifix in the East window and that Muttet & Birch were at the same tyme at Church & heard the words, & hee & Mathew Birch came into the towne to dwell together. And to this they offer further witnesses, as also to his words herein charged, nor will they be rimed out of their knowledge & memory by blessinge for better & curse for worse, neither will Mathew Birch yeild to be thrust out of the parish by his sly allegation but saith that he was present & heard the very words.

13) To the 13th the deponents do iustify this charge. One of them, John Bacon, was then att Coddenham in his company & protesteth that the vicar dranke a lusty deale of liquor at that tyme, & was very apish after it in his cariage & demeanor. And that his horse (if possible) might speake to this article, which was putt to the heyt above ordinary & could not but be sensible of some swayes of the vicar's body.

14) To the 14th the vicar understandeth not "disguised"; I feare the playne English "drunke" wilbe home proved. He would recriminate & doth it in riddles; our playnnesse cannott expound them. Bonham saith he knoweth not what he meanes by that cloake, unlesse it be the foolish mistake of his maid servant, who because he came into his chamber (he havinge layd it off in another room before) without his cloke, supposed it had been lost & sent one out unknown to her Master to seeke for it. He hath often slept in an Inne (& useth to sleepe every afternoone in the yeere) sometymes wearyed with travayle by the fireside. And once had adventured to sleepe

[1] James Buck, Vicar of Stradbroke: his case appears in the *Century* (No. 86). He was charged with preaching 'popish' doctrine – including that the Pope was head of the Church, with subscribing to the Laudian ceremonial innovations, and with expressing great malignancy against the Parliament.

upon a bedd if the vicar would have given way. In short he prayeth he may never be so debauched as he was once in this vicar's company; he never was so badd before, neither then was he worse then the vicar himselfe, which surely the vicar cannott forgett, no more then the callinge for the Cragge of stronge drinke to be brought upp into his owne roome at Boxford (indeed this was a good way to putt downe an alehouse, to tipple upp all the good drinke himselfe), no more then he can forgett the notable bout att Hadleigh to prepare him for the service of the next, which was a fast day. I could say much of this kind, but I had rather lend him a peice of the lost cloke to cover his foule shame, then imitate him in this fault or putt in practize his Jesu-iticall maxime *Audaciter Calummando semper aliquid haret:* a loud lye leaves a deepe print.

(*Added later in the margin.*) Robert Bacon deposeth that he saw the vicar drinke a great deale of strong beer & wyne att Coddenham wherewith he was so much distempered that goeing home he reeled many tymes out of the path & twice into certen plashes of water & had two severall falls before he recovered his house.

15) To the 15th, for his appeale herein to his other neighbours in the parish wee have replyed in the preface. His frequent invectives against the Parliament theis deponents will iustifie. And Mr Beale must pardon them for so longe as they remember themselves to be English-men they will not forgett to love & defend an English Parliament. They request that one Edward Turner of Ash may be strictly examyned concerning this point of this Article. (*Added in the margin.* John Bacon & one Robert Brooke were ready to charge this Edward Turner with what he had heard the Parson say in this matter, but Edward Turner would not appeare before the Committee.) How litle tyme he bestoweth in good studyes they do know, as easily they may by his often iornyes & ramblinge about, and into what companyes, but of the most desperate Malignants both Clergy & lay of all others. I would know, in all his tyme so vainely spent, what faithfull Minister he ever repayred unto or what other godly company he ever frequented. For his good service of the parish wee confesse it hath been badd heretofore; what then, shall wee not partake of the benifitt of Reformation now in theis dayes of reformation? Sueringe & Citeinge is no part of the Charge, yett to that wee answer there was good reason hee should make no trouble when he could not; the blessed Parliament (I feare Mr Beale meaneth that at Oxford) was to looke after theis popish oppressions iust upon the vicar's first comeinge, yett wee can prove that in that narrow interim he threatned to overthrow the Customes of the towne which he called Develish, because they touched the monke's belly, and kept the silken pettycoate for embracing their females' loynes.

16, 17, 18.) To the 16:17:18 the deponents reply to theis answers that Mr Bonham being certified that the vicar had not taken the Covenant before the Committee (as was directed by the ordinance) deemed the vicar dis-abled to give it to the parish and expected some other to be appointed to minister it; this made him go out of the Church then. But one William Alderton craftily and falsely affirminge that Mr Beale had dispensation from the Committee to take it with his neighbours, Mr Bonham retorned & tooke it presently. They are likewise ready to iustify the 17th Article. And Bonham affirmeth for himselfe that if he had seen the vicar but endeavour to give reasons for the three things in this Article charged, how weake soever they had been he should have accepted them & thought the man a Convertite (so great is his pride & subtilty). And Bonham saith that the rather he expected those reasons to be by him assigned, because he had often heard the vicar solemnely vow heretofore that he would voluntarily depart into exile and never retorne into the bosom of the Church of England if ever Episcopacy were deposed here; and this Bonham's wife is able to iustify upon her oath. Likewise the 18th they affirme and appeale to the practize of all the faithfull Ministers in the Country.

Matthew Birch; Thomas Grymwade: Hereunto they add new Articles against the vicar, that since theis Articles exhibited he hath taken on him the spirit of prophecy and foretelleth in the pulpitt the restoringe those men of parts, those great stares to their owne Orbs (vizt., the eiected Ministers), sayeing he knew to what party he spake. Bidding not to mourne for their want after the mourneinge of Rachell, for the tyme was att hand & not a farr off. And this wee humbly hope he borrowed of the Spirit that rose from under the throne, and beinge so inspired he wants but a paire of hornes to his head and he shall grace & buffett the true prophetts.

Finally Bacon & Birch, if they hired land of Mr Bonham they provided for their owne indempnity so that the vicar's testimony against Bonham would in no wise do them any preiudice; lett him then bethinke him of some new ground for so grosse a periury as he layeth to their charge, which, if he can assigne none reasonable, they challenge the good opinions of good men, the rest they weigh not.

June 23rd 1644 he said in his sermon that they were the flowers of the garden that now were rooted upp. (Witnesses: Thomas Bonham, Matthew Birch.)

Sunday 21st July 1644 he said in his sermon Us that are the successors of the Apostles they thrust out of the Ministry; but however the wretchednes & wickednes of theis present tymes do persecute us, we are bound to preach the gospell.

This Replication was brought in July 23 1644, and delivered upon oath. Mr Beale being present doth deny the 3 last Articles & every tittle of them.

Proved before Nathaniel Bacon, William Bloys, Peter Fisher, Robert Duncon, John Base.

Manchester issued a warrant for his ejection on the 30th July 1644, directing it to the Suffolk Committee for Scandalous Ministers.

Articles against John Beadle, Rector of Trimley St. Martin.

I. That the said Beadle is a conformist to Bishopp Wren's popish & superstitious Innovations; he hath bowed at the name of Jesus, kneeled & bowed before the rayles. (John Hart,*[1] Samuel Cortnall*).

[1] An asterisk against the name of a witness signifies that he also testified against John Ferror, Rector of Trimley St Mary. (See below, p. 71.)

II. The said Beadle hath absented himselfe from his cure & flocke full twenty weekes in a yeere. After he had gott his offringe the last Easter he absented himselfe for 5 weekes, also after he had gott in his tithes at harvest he absented himselfe at least 5 weekes. He hath also absented himselfe since before the fast in February untill this fifteenth of Aprill, not providinge any other to supply his roome so that his flocke hath been left destitute of a pastor, a fitt prey for wolves to devoure. (Samuel Cortnall,* John King,* John Hawyes, Robert Sword).

III. The said Beadle hath refused to associate, sayeing it went against his conscience, & did disherten his neighbours from it not only in his example, but by his verball dehortations. (William Blackman,* John Hawyes, John King*).

IV. The said Beadle hath refused to read & publish any ordinance of Parliament that theis could ever observe for 3 yeeres past, or to obey them in any wise. He would not pay what he was assessed untill he was distreyned. (Samuel Cortnall,* John Hawyes).

V. Lastly the said Beadle doth utterly refuse to take either of the covenants, sayeinge he would rather be puld in peics then to take them. (Francis Daniel, Samuel Cortnall*).

That the said Beadle is now gon quite away, and the voice goeth he hath resignd to Sir John Barker; but for some reasons which we can alledge if we be called wee do humbly pray that this Committee would be pleased to nominate Samuel Bache, Master of Arts, to the right honourable the Earle of Manchester to be Minister to both the Tremleys, the Churches standinge in one Churchyard. (John Gayford,* Samuel Cortnall*).

Aprill 15th 1644: theis Articles were proved before us, Nathaniel Bacon, Francis Brewster, Nathaniel Bacon, William Bloys, Robert Duncon, Peter Fisher.

Manchester issued a warrant for his ejection on the 8th July 1644, directing it to Samuel Courtnall, John King and William Hales.

Articles against Edmund Mayor, Rector of Finningham, taken at Diss on the 6th June 1644.

I. Inprimis Edmund Coleman gent, John Frere gent, and Thomas Preston of Fynningham aforesaid & Thomas Rust gent of Rickingale superior do say upon their oathes that the said Mr Mayor doth usually preach but once a day, and hath neglected catechizinge a longe tyme, and when he preacheth he readeth constantly that he seemeth to preach.

II. Item John Grocer senior of West Thorpe & Joseph Bedwall and Robert Brett of Fynningham aforesaid do say upon their oathes that the said Mr Mayor hath been a comon haunter or frequenter of Innes, Alehouses & Tiplinghouses.

III. Item George Osborne of Fynningham aforesaid & Ellen Yongs of Gislingham do say upon their oathes that the said Mr Mayor with two or

D

three more about two or three yeeres since did buy a vessell of beere which was brought to a neighbour's house in the towne where they did drinke out the same, and more to a good quantity. At which tyme he with some of the rest that were with him were so distempered with drinkeinge that they fell out amonge themselves, and one of them then receyved a hurt thereby.

IV. Item the said Joseph Bedwall and Susan his wife do say upon their oathes that one Elizabeth Webster who lyved with the said Mr Mayor in his parsonage hath reported in their hearinge that the said Mr Mayor hath been so distempered with drinkinge that her husband was fayne to guid him home & helpe him to bedd.

Item: the 5th & 6th Articles not proved.

VII. Item the said Robert Brett & Edmond Coleman & Robert Webster of Fynningham afforesaid do say upon their oathes that the said Mr Mayor hath been very forward in observation of Bishopp Wren's superstitious Iniunctions, as bowinge at the name of Jesus & reading the second service at the high Alter or Comunion table railed in at the East end of the Chancell, and caused his parishioners to come upp to the rayle to receyve the sacrament.

VIII. Item Robert Browne of Fynningham doth say upon his oath that the said Mr Mayor when the rayles were taken upp and the Comunion table brought downe from the East end of the Chancell according to an order of one or both houses of parliament, he, with the helpe of the Sexton or some other, sett it upp agayne, sayeing there it should stand.

IX. Item the said Thomas Preston & George Osbourne of Fynningham aforesaid do say upon their oathes that the said Mr Mayor being at a neighbour's house, in the said house, there being some speech about the Parliament, tooke bread & said to one there present that as that was bread the king had had the better of it all this tyme, whatsoever was reported. And that for his part his daily prayer was for the Kinge, that God in heaven would increase his forces.

X. Item the said George Osborne doth say upon his oath that the said Mr Mayor, soone after the last election of knights of the shire in Suffolk, confessed that he being at the king's head att Ipswich, where Sir Nathaniel Barnardiston[1] lodged, had used speeches to this effect, that if a dogge which did then come upp there had been a Barnardiston he would have knockt him on the head.

XI. Item the said John Frere & Edmond Coleman do say upon their oathes that the said Mr Mayor hath been backward in contributinge to the Parliament; for he did give but 20/– upon the first propositions that wee ever heard of.

XII. Item the said Joseph Bedwall & John Luff of Fynningham do say upon their oathes that the said Mr Mayor's horse being taken by troopers by reason of his disafection to the Parliament, he did give out distastfull &

---

[1] Sir Nathaniel Barnardiston of Kedington (1588–1653), Knight of the Shire for Suffolk in the Long Parliament. For a comment on his local position and influence, see Everitt, op. cit., pp. 18–21. For the Suffolk election for the Long Parliament, see my thesis, op. cit., pp. 43–6.

threatininge speeches, and said he would lay felony to them if they came agayne.

XIII. Item the said George Osborne doth say upon his oath that the said Mr Mayor hath sometyme neglected the celebration of some fast dayes, and when he doth keepe any he preacheth but once a day; and hath been heard to sweare by his troath he could not preach.

XIV. Item the said Edmond Coleman & Thomas Preston do say upon their oathes that the said Mr Mayor hath taught that a man may be saved by faith onely without good workes, and instanced for prooffe the theif upon the Crosse.

XV. Item the said Edmond Coleman & Robert Barker of Finningham aforesaid do say upon their oathes that the said Mr Mayor hath refused to read bookes or ordinancs which have been sent from the Parliament and appointed to be read.

XVI. Item the said Edmond Coleman & George Osborne do say upon their oathes that the said Mr Mayor would not upon the readinge of the writinge or order for contribution to the right honourable the Lord Fairfax exhort the parishioners to a cheerefull benevolence, although required by warrant, and refused to give any thinge himselfe.

XVII. Item the said Edmond Coleman & Robert Brett do say upon their oathes that the said Mr Mayor, when the ordinance was sent unto him for raisinge of moneye for the Scott's advance, would not read the same publickly nor make any exhortation concerninge it although he had a warrant to do the same.

XVIII. Item the said George Osborne doth say upon his oath that the said Mr Mayor shortly after the begininge of this Parliament used deriding speeches concerning Sir Nathaniel Barnardiston to the effect followinge (vizt) That all the other knights & gentlemen had made speeches there, but all the speech that he had made was Sirs, shutt the doore least wee gett could.

XIX. Item the said Robert Barker doth say upon his oath that the said Mr Mayor, about Christmas last was a twelvemoneth, hath been heard say that if theis troubles were not ended by our Lady [*i.e. Lady Day – the 25th March.*] he would not give 5/– for Sir Edmond Bacon his estate.[1]

XX. Item Nicholas Martyn & Edmond Albone of Walsham do say upon their oathes that the said Mr Mayor hath not been only forward in his owne parish to performe what hath beene required by the Bishopps' Iniunctions, but he once went to Walsham and there pronounced excomunication against Abigail Margery, the wife of Raph Margery, who was a godly pious matron (which the Minister of the parish would not do himselfe); and caused her to be carried out of the Church, and after prayers were read, [*she*] comminge agayne into the Church, he asked what that excomunicated woman did

[1] Sir Edmund Bacon, Bart., of Redgrave Hall. He was one of the wealthiest men in Suffolk at this period. (See A. Simpson, *The Wealth of the Gentry*, Cambridge 1961, pp. 94–5.)

there, and caused her agayne to be putt out and would not suffer her to heare the sermon.[1]

XXI. Item the said John Frere, Edmund Coleman, Thomas Rust, John Grocer, Joseph Bedwall, Robert Barker, & Robert Webster & John Knyvett of Fynningham afforesaid do say upon their oathes that the said Mr Mayor is one that taketh litle paynes in his studyes, and seemeth very unable to discharge that callinge in our iudgements.

XXII. Item the said John Webster, John Knyvett & John Luff do say upon their oathes that the said Mr Mayor hath so farr tollerated ordinary workinge upon the fast day, that upon a fast day in Harvest was twelvemoneth he gave Shearers of corne of his mother in lawe in the said towne a larges after they had donn.

XXIII. Item the said Edmond Coleman doth say upon his oath that the said Mr Mayor, although he were desired by this deponent to make an exhortation to his parishioners concerninge the nationall covenant before the takinge thereof in his parish to stirr them upp to a willing taking thereof, he would not do the same, though he was enioyned thereunto by order or instructions of Parliament.

XXIV. Item the said Joseph Bedwall & Robert Brett do say upon their oathes that the said Mr Mayor did never reprove any for prophaninge of the Lord's day to any of our knowledges although he seeth some often prophane the same day by sports in his parish.

XXV. Item the said Edmund Coleman, Joseph Bedwall and Thomas Preston do say upon their oathes that the said Mr Mayor doth commonly keepe company with such men as are ill affected to the Parliament & their proceedings.

XXVI. Item the said Joseph Bedwall & Robert Brett do say upon their oathes that the said Mr Mayor doth frequently use to sweare, bann & curse in his comunication.

XXVII. Item the said Joseph Bedwall & Robert Brett do say upon their oathes that the said Mr Mayor is stronge to drinke, & being drinkinge in a company many houres together hath pressed some to drinke a whole pott that have refused it.

XXVIII. Item the said Joseph Bedwall & Susan his wife, Robert Brett and Martha his wife do say upon their oathes that the said Mr Mayor hath drawne some of his neighbours to sitt so longe drinkinge togeither that their wifes have been fayne to leave them & go home without them.

XXIX. Item the said George Osborne, Thomas Preston & Joseph Bedwall do say upon their oathes that the said Mr Mayor hath said in his preachinge that if a man kept the bible in his house it would keepe the devill out of his house, or words to that purpose.

[1] For Margery, see note 1 on page 30. The persecution of Margery and his wife by the religious authorities in the 1630s was discussed in Parliament in 1641. (See W. Notestein (ed.), *The Journal of Sir Simonds D'Ewes, from the beginning of the Long Parliament to the Opening of the trial of the Earl of Strafford*, New Haven 1923, p. 398.)

The Rectory is worth £50 per annum, and besides this Mayor has a temporal estate of £50 per annum. Mayor is married, and has one child.

6th June 1644: Proved before Tobias Frere, Henry Kinge, Robert Gooch, John Greenwood, Thomas Lincoln.

Manchester issued the warrant for the ejection of Mayor on the 8th July, directing it to Samuel Jorden, Elias Stamm, William Rye, and Henry Howlett.

Articles against Mark Reynolds, Rector of Wixoe.

I. The said Mr Reynolds hath practised all the late Innovations, as administringe the Sacrament at the alter & rayles, & bowinge towards the Comunion table.

II. After he had been before the Committee in Cambridge, at his retorne home, in his sermon after a railinge manner he enveighed against the honourable assemblyes of Parliament, sayeinge they had now the better of the kinge, for they had gott his hand & seale and now they would have his crowne; boastinge further in the said sermon that when he was with the Committees his townesmen durst not give in evidence against him.

III. (*left blank*)

IV. At another tyme he was heard to say that the Parliament might as well pull downe the Churches as the pictures in them, for they were sett upp by the same power & authority.

V. He hath inveighed against some people that did goe abroad to heare godly Ministers, sayeing that they went to heare seditious fellowes and which did preach their owne Inventions, no true doctrine; and therein they were like to litle children running after a redd apple. And in particuler he said of one Mr Richard Blackeby & Mr Samuel Fairecloth, two reverend Ministers neer to us, that they were seditious Ministers, & troublers of the Commonwealth.[1]

---

[1] There are articles on both Samuel Fairclough (1594–1677) and Richard Blackerby (1574–1648) in D.N.B. The latter, although he published nothing, was one of the most influential Puritan ministers of his generation; Samuel Clarke described him as 'one of the holiest men on earth'. Having been ejected from the living of Feltwell (Norfolk) for nonconformity he settled at Ashen where he educated 'a great number of Youths, the Sons of Pious Gentry, Tradesmen, and Yeomen in the Country'. Besides teaching, Blackerby also lectured frequently, and in this respect his residence at Ashen had the advantage of being near the borders of three dioceses; 'if he were suspended in one . . . he would go and preach in another.' Fairclough had been one of his pupils, and was to become his son-in-law; he was minister of Kedington, to which living he was appointed by Sir Nathaniel Barnardiston who actively protected him from persecution during the Laudian regime. Indeed during the 1630s the area about Kedington became an island of seigneurial Puritanism, standing out against the prevailing ecclesiastical tendencies; 'there was one grat advantage which this Town and Corner had above most other places, and that was this, That the Magistracy and Ministry joined both together, and concurred in all things for promoting of true Piety and Godliness. The countenance and encouragement which a man of great Estate and Power doth give to a Minister is of great import and influence upon his Ministry'. There are very interesting biographies of both men in S. Clarke, *The Lives of Sundry Eminent Persons in this Later Age* (1683), from which the quotations in this note are taken.

VI. He hath been divers tymes drunke; and also he did oppose Mr Blackeby a reverend preacher who by the parishioners of Ashen was intreated to preach at their towne & he went from his owne towne, & when he the said Marke Reynolds had read prayers & the psalme sung Mr Blackeby went into the pulpett to preach, and he would not suffer him, but in the deske he did begin & made Mr Blackeby come downe.

VII. He did frequently bow toward the Communion table & preached against the last covenant and disswaded some from taking it and hath exercised great malignancy against the Parliament & filleth aswell his sermons as his ordnary discourses with bitter invectives & slanders against Godly Ministers and those that are religiously affected.

VIII. Upon discouse of one Mr Brewer of Castle Heningham in Essex, about a godly sermon he preached at Clare which caused much ioy; [*he*] sayeing it was a ioyfull thinge that godly Ministers are now in request, and noiatinge Mr Fayrecloth, Mr Blackeby & Mr Burwell[1] who once had their mouthes stopped, but now, god be praised, they had liberty to preach the gospell freely, to which the said Mr Marke Reynolds answered that the said Mr Fayrecloth, Mr Blackeby and Mr Burwell were rebells & did not teach the written word of god.

IX. He said that those of the Parliament are in a wronge way of proceedinge for the establishinge of peace & religion in the Commonwealth, and he said [*they*] sate for their owne ends.

X. He said that itis pitty those be suffered that do speake against Bishopps & their Bishoppricks and of their hierarchy in Ecclesiasticall governement in Church & Commonwealth.

XI. He said that those who are called by the name of Cavaliers that remayne with the kinge are in the right way for reformation, and that the Parliament is in the wronge way.

XII. That the Reverend Bishopps, as he termed them, have not wisedome enough to establishe Religion, but every layman or rather every foole must give their advice to the worke, or else they will sat itis nothinge worth.

3 May, 20th Charles I: Depositions taken before Francis Bacon Esq., Sir William Spring Bt., Sir William Soame, Robert Brewster, Thomas Tirrell Esqs., Francis Brewster, gent.

---

[1] Edmund Brewer was minister of Castle Hedingham; in the 1630s he was constantly in trouble with the authorities for his hostility to Laudianism. The Reverend Harold Smith, in his *The Ecclesiastical History of Essex under the Long Parliament and Commonwealth* (Colchester, no date), prints many of the official complaints against him (see pp. 40, 44–5, 49, 53). Christopher Burrell, another pupil and son-in-law of Blackerby, was presented to Great Wratting by Sir Nathaniel Barnardiston. Early in Wren's episcopate he publicly protested against his 'superstitious innovations', and was deprived (see S.P. 18/76/7). At the beginning of the Long Parliament Lady Anne Barnardiston wrote to Sir Simonds D'Ewes informing him that unless her son, Sir Nathaniel, speedily got Burrell restored to his living he would be censured by 'those of the best ranke, according to God's account'. (Harl. 384, f. 27.)

Witnesses; to the truth of the
1st Article – *Nicholas Gilvin, Henry Smith.*
2nd Article – *Nicholas Gilvin.*
4th Article – *Daniel Wade.*
5th Article – *Henry Smith, Nicholas Gilvin, Jonathan Paske.*
6th Article – *Edward Sams, Joseph Dowse, Mary Ager, Elizabeth Chaplin, John Pledger, Thomas Edwards.*
7th Article – *Nicholas Gilvin, Henry Smith.*
8th Article – *John Powell.*
9th Article – *John Chaplin, and Elizabeth his wife.*
To the 10th, 11th and 12th Articles they cannot depose.

Mary Ager was examined on the 28th June 1644 by the direction of the Earl of Manchester, before Thomas Tirrell, Edmund Harvey, Thomas Chaplin, Brampton Gurdon and Nathaniel Bacon.

Manchester issued his warrant for the ejection of Reynolds on the 28th July, directing it to Nicholas Gilvin, Daniel Wade, John Powell, and Thomas Smith.

Articles against Nicholas Coleman, Rector of Preston.

I. He is popishly affected, being an observer of sondry Innovations & ceremonyes & also bowing at his mentioning the name 'Jesus', and usinge & holdinge much with the crosse in baptisme.

II. That he hath given out in speeches that they were all blockheads & beetleheads that spake against the crosse in baptisme.

III. Whereas some of his well-affected neighbours desired him first to take the vow & covenant sett forth by the Parliament the last summer, he said if he should take it he should damne his soule. And further said he would not advise any of his parishioners to take the covenant, for, [he] said, your blood shalbe required at my hands. And moreover he puld out the king's declaration & read it in the Church to discourage the well affected people that were there intentionally to take the same covenant. Likewise he said that all those that did take the covenant were traytors against the kinge.

IV. That he never kept any day of thanksgivinge accordinge to the Parliament's direction, by reason whereof his parishioners were enforced to go to other parishes to keepe those dayes. And he seldome or never gave his parishioners notice of the fast dayes before they came, or excite or stirr them upp to prepare their hearts for the solemne dutyes of those fast dayes.

V. He is much given to reproach & scandalize godly & painefull Ministers, by name Mr Fayrecloth of Ketton & Mr Smith of Cuckfeild,[1] sayeing he would take his oath that Mr Fairecloth preached false doctryne, and hearinge

---

[1] John Smith, Rector of Cockfield, to which living he was presented by Sir William Spring. Coleman's comment may not have been wide of the mark: Smith gave no trouble to the Laudian authorities, and was to retain his living after 1660.

that Mr Smith did stirre upp & quicken his parishioners to take the Covenant above mentioned he made answer that the said Mr Smith would observe anythinge, and would turne as the wind or wethercocke.

VI. He is most scandalous in his life, being a frequent company keeper and very much given to drinkinge, and sometymes hath been so overcome with beere that he hath been necessarily guided home. And on Ashwensday last was twelvemonethes, he being overgone with beere, did either breake his legg or putt it out of ioynt, and in that humor desired the bonesetter to sett his legg in such manner that he might goe on it agayne the next morninge – although it was six weekes after at least before he could shew himselfe at his Church after that miscariage.

VII. He is one that in his common discourse doth usually sweare by his faith & troth.

VIII. He said that the Parliament was the cause of all theis troubles, for he said that they did deny the Kinge his right and kept from him his prerogative which would be a meanes to spoile all. And he never lookt to see peace till wee be all killed.

Depositions taken the 14th June 1644 before Sir William Spring, Maurice Barrow, Nathaniel Bacon of Friston, William Bloys, Brampton Gurdon jnr., Edmund Harvey, Samuel Moody, Thomas Chaplin.

Witnesses to the truth of the
1st Article – *John Barker, Edmund Pannell.*
2nd Article – *Henry Ranson.*
3rd Article – *John Barker, Elias Stoneham, Edward Rauson, Henry Howlett.*
4th Article – *Elias Stoneham, Edward Rauson, Edmund Pannell, Henry Howlett.*
5th Article – *Henry Howlett and Susan his wife.*
6th Article – *Henry Howlett, William Howe, Edmund Pannell, John Wright depose that they know that the said Mr Coleman doth keepe very idle and vayne company, and that they have seen him at severall tymes drunke.*
7th Article – *Samuel Jorden, Edmund Pannell, Elias Stoneham.*
8th Article – *John Barker.*

Manchester issued the warrant for his ejection on the 23rd July 1644, directing it to Edward Coleman, Thomas Preston, Robert Barker and Joseph Bedall.

Articles against William Walker, Vicar of Winston, examined by the Committee sitting at Ipswich on the 1st April 1644.

I. The said William Walker doth affirme and maynteyn that the papists be as good orthodox Divines and as pious & godly as wee, bowing to Images only excepted. (Richard Moysy, Bridget Philips).

II. The said Mr Walker is very superstitious in his practices in cringing &

boweing to the Communion table sett upp at the East end of the Chancell. Both affirme his preaching for the boweinge at the name of Jesus & practizinge the same. (Mary Jaques, Thomas Glamfield).

III. The said Mr Walker forced his parishioners to receyve the sacrament at the rayles (sett before the table at the east end of the chancell), and did putt by divers of his parishioners from recevinge because they would not receyve at the said rayles. (George Jaques).

IV. The said Mr Walker being requested by one of his parishioners that he might receyve the sacrament as he had formerly donn, Mr Walker answered he would speake with his freind Mr Hoalt concerninge it, and George Jaques saith that Mr Hoalt was a popish parson. Nicholas Giles saeing [*that*] Mr Walker in a rage said in theis words, By the helpe of my god the Lord Bishopp he should know of this. (Henry Smith, George Jaques).

V. The said Mr Walker is a grosse prophaner of the lord's day by draweing his parishioners to reckoning with him and taking of money on that day, and also frequently to take iournyes then & thereby neglect the charge of his parish. (John Banyard, Richard Moysy).

VI. The said Mr Walker did much applaud the Bishopps for reverend fathers, and the Earle of Newcastle for a zealous protestant, and that he is accounted for a puritan. Edmund Heursant saith that Mr Walker much applauded Bishop Laud. (John Banyard, Isaac Philips, Richard Moysy).

VII. The said Mr Walker publickly in his preachinge rayled upon our brethren the Scotts upon their first comminge, calling them Rebells; & their cominge over is to ravish mens' wives & to deflower virgins. (John Banyard, Henry Smith, George Jaques).

VIII. The said Mr Walker hath been a common hanter of tavernes & alehouses at unseasonable tymes; saith he saw him once out of the Angell taverne by 4 of the clocke in the morninge upon saturday neer Christmas. (Richard Shepherd, James Philips, John Warde).

IX. The said Mr Walker is reported to be a common drunkerd and hath been oftentimes seene to be drunken, to stagger in the streets, and not able to go without leadinge. (John Warde, James Philips, Richard Shepherd, John Denant, John True, John Peake).

X. The said Mr Walker did at his drunken meeting drinke a health to Prince Rupert att an alehouse or Inne; he did begin the said cursed health, & forced the same upon the rest of the company. (William Thompson).

XI. The said Mr Walker is a great & comon gamster at tables for money, & hath wonne & lost much money. (George Jaques, Isaac Philips, Richard Moysy).

XII. The said Mr Walker hath had much disorder at his house by playeinge as aforesaid, and also by excessive drinkinge and great resort of evill affected persons daily to his house. Richard Moysy saith that Mr Walker plaid at tables all night before the fast about a yeere since. (John Banyard, Isaac Philips).

XIII. The said Mr Walker doth much insult at the losse of the Parliament's forcs and att the victoryes & good successes of the Cavaleers. (Richard Moysy, Isaac Philips).

XIV. The said Mr Walker commonly praieth that the lord would make it manifest which side doth stand for the truth. (Richard Moysy, Isaac Philips).

XV. The said Mr Walker hath been backward upon all the propositions of Parliament and averse to other the Parliament's ordinancs. (Richard Shepherd, Richard Moysy, Isaac Philips).

XVI. The said Mr Walker did not take the first covenant but according to his owne invention; and being asked whether he had sett his hand to the same he answered in a great rage, sayeing before he would take it without limitation he would be drawne in peics with horses or be burnt at a stake or suffer imprisonement, and thereby much hindred the takinge of it by others. (George Jaques, Edward Heaward, Henry Smith, Isaac Philips).

Proved on oath before Nathaniel Bacon, William Bloys, Francis Bacon, Robert Brewster, Peter Fisher, John Base.

A Replication to Walker's answer, presented to the Committee sitting at Ipswich on the 2nd July.

Whereas Mr Walker in his answer saith that if he would have given £5 they would have desisted from the prosecution of the said articles: that they being at Bury, money was spoken of to give to beare the witinesses chardges, to which they replyed that it was no money matter that they stood upon but a recantation sermon & two yeeres experience of him for his amendment, to which they had often admonished him, telling him that a man of his parts could not be longe without a place if he carryed himself and other words to that effect. (George Jaques, Richard Sharpe, Edmund Heursant, Isaac Philips).

That they have seen him drunke & often distempered with beere or wyne, not being able to guide himselfe in his goeinge. (Richard Shepherd, James Philips).

That about a yeere since he did see him disguised with drinke or wyne. (Thomas Reader, John Goddard).

That in March last he was so distempered with beere or wyne that he could not guide himselfe. (Richard Whitinge).

That they heard Mr Walker say that wee may see which side God takes part withall, for all the money in the land is litle enough to maynteyn the Parliament; and the Lord doth assist the Kinge out of the dust of the earth. (Samuel Moysy, Susan Philips).

That he sent for him on a lord's day to pay the said Mr Walker 12d which he said was due to him for a harth henn, and for churchinge the said Banyard's wife; which the said Mr Banyard refusing, the said Mr Walker said Sirrah, you will do worse. (John Banyard).

That the said Mr Walker did usually bow towards the communion table standing within the rayles. (John Banyard, John Goddard).

That he frequently used & suffred to be used in his house gameinge & drinkinge excessively. (John Banyard, Isaac Philips).

That he hath seen Mr Walker lose above 12/– at one tyme at gameinge. (Isaac Philips).

That Robert Cracknell being sicke & upon his deathbed did severall tymes say that if it would please god to restore him to his health, he, the said Cracknell, would endeavor that Mr Walker should be punished for his drunkennes; by which wee concyve that the said Cracknell was not greived for taxinge the said Mr Walker for drunkennes as Mr Walker alleadgeth in his answer. (Richard Whitinge, George Jaques).

That Ward & Durrant, accused by Mr Walker, are of honest report & religious men, and cleere from the aspersion laid upon them, as they herd Mr Smith confesse that there was no such matter, and he never accused them of any such thinge as taking of the turkyes. (Richard Whitinge, John Banyard, John Goddard).

Proved before: Nathaniel Bacon, William Bloys, Robert Duncon, Peter Fisher, John Base.

Manchester issued his warrant for Walker's ejection on the 7th August 1644, directing it to Isaac Phillips, Edward Harsant, George Jacques.

Articles against Edward Key, Rector of Sotherton: proved the 20th June 1644 before the Committee sitting at Yoxford.

I. The said Mr Key is a common swearer, and doth sweare by his faith & troth and by the name of god. (Thomas Hassell, Alice Hassell).

II. He is a companion of malignants & other loose & disordered persons, and doth frequent alehouses – as namely the houses of Thomas Pightelyn & Ellis and others. (Robert Freeman, Thomas Hassell).

III. He hath conformed himselfe to all Bishopp Wren's iniunctions, as namely to bow before the communion table 2 or 3 severall tymes at his goeing upp to the rayles, to bow at the mentioning the name of Jesus, to preach in his surplice & tippett, to stand upp at Gloria patri, & frequently to read the second service at the rayles. (Thomas Hassell, Robert Freeman, Robert Chapman, Robert Lilly, Henry Barrow).

IV. He hath preached many severall sermons within the rayles. (Thomas and Alice Hassell, Robert Chapman, Robert Freeman, Henry Barrow[1]).

V. He hath presented some of his parishioners, as namely Thomas Heaseall & Alice his wife, for their not comminge to the rayles to receyve the

---

[1] The names of Thomas and Alice Hassell were subsequently erased as witnesses to this article.

sacrament; and did prosecute the said presentement unto an excommunication & a significavit.[1] (Thomas and Alice Hassell).

VI. He did sweare by the name of god that he would never administer the sacrament of the lord's supper while he lived unto the said Thomas Heaseall unles he would come upp to the rayles for the same. And Alice Heasall testifieth that he swore by his faith that he would not admitt her husband, the said Thomas Hasell to the sacrament though he lived in that place 7 yeeres; sayeing that he would never change his wise, for he never worshiped God so holily, godly & divinely as now, and god never receyved so much honor as he did since this way of worshipe came upp. (Thomas and Alice Hassell).

The parsonage is worth £30 a year; he is also Rector of Tunstall-cum-Dunningworth, worth £60 a year. Key is unmarried, and has no personal estate.

Proved before: Nathaniel Bacon, Nathaniel Bacon, Peter Fisher, Robert Brewster, Francis Brewster, John Base.

Manchester's warrant ejecting Key is undated and undirected.

Articles against William Raymond, Rector of Blyford:[2] proved before the Committee at Yoxford on the 20th June 1644.

I. The said Mr Raymond is a common swearer by faith & troth and sometimes by the name of god; and Alice Hasell testifieth that she being att dinner with him once heard him sweare 18 severall times by his faith & troth or by the name of god. (Phineas Swett, Thomas Hassell, Thomas Green).

II. He is a common drunkerd and Alice Hasell testifieth that he once cominge to baptize a child was soe distempered with drinke that he could not hold the child or give a right pronunciation of the words concerning baptisme, the company then being forced to send for him from the alehouse at Halsworth. And Susan Ellis testifieth that upon the fast day, being the 27th of March last, he wholly neglected his cure and came that night from an Alehouse at Halsworth (the house of one Edmond Browne) to the house of one John Feveryeare of Holton so drunken that she being then servant there dared not to abide in the house with him, he swering there commonly in his talke. (Phineas Swett, Thomas Hassell, Thomas Green).

III. He hath absented himselfe from his cure by the space of 16 weekes or thereabouts, none but malignant persons supplieing the cure in his absence. (Thomas and Alice Hassell, Thomas Slath).

[1] Writ out of Chancery issued on certificate by the Bishop of a man standing excommunicate for 40 days; the writ authorised the imprisonment of the offender until he submitted to the ecclesiastical court.

[2] According to a correspondent of John Walker's (Ms. J. Walker, c. 5, f. 85) Raymond was a preacher of considerable repute, and after his sequestration a group of local gentlemen allowed him to preach in their houses, where his ex-parishioners came to hear him. This arrangement came to the ears of Miles Corbett, the M.P. for Yarmouth, who promised Raymond that, if he would come to London, he would procure an order from the Committee allowing him to preach. However, when Raymond appeared before the Committee, Corbett denounced him and he was forbidden to preach again. I have found nothing to confirm this story in the records of the Committee of Plundered Ministers.

IV. That he is a frequent player at cards & dice & bowles. (John Painton, Robert Ladbrooke, the constable).

V. That the Constables goeinge to imprest a man for the service of kinge & Parliament about 10 weekes since went to an unlicensed alehouse to see what company there was, where they found divers, among whom was Mr Raymond, it being between 10 or 11 of the clocke at night. Where they charginge a man to go alonge with them, the said Mr Raymond rescued him from the Constable, &, in the reskue, gave one of the Constables a rush upon his brest whereappon he raised blood the next day and hath languished ever since & is yett in much danger. (Thomas Tredescant, Robert Ladbrooke).

The parsonage is worth £40–50 a year; his personal estate will be worth £40–50 a year upon the death of his mother.

Day was given to Mr Raymond to putt in his defence to the 8th of July, but he brought in no answer.

Proved before: Nathaniel Bacon, Nathaniel Bacon, Peter Fisher, Robert Brewster, Francis Brewster, John Base.

Manchester's warrant for the ejection of Raymond is undated and undirected.

Articles against Thomas Newman, Rector of Little Cornard.

I. That the said Mr Newman was a strict observer of Bishopp Wren's Iniunctions, bowing at the naminge of the word 'Jesus', and usually when he went to read the second service at the comunion table he made low obedience towards the said table by bowinge his body. (Robert Nutt, Jeffrey Peach, William Walters, Peter Lay, William Long).

II. That Mr Newman, untill his late Curate came to him, never preached but once upon the saboth dayes, and his sermons for the most parte were to rebuke those his wellaffected parishioners that went to other Churches to heare the word preached. (Henry Underwood, Richard Robinson, Robert Nutt, Jeffrey Peach, Peter Lay, William Walters, William Long).

III. That he never to their knowledge catechiseth any of his parishioners, either yong or old in the grounds of religion but receiveth all to the sacrament of the lord's supper though never so prophane in their lives. (Richard Robinson, Henry Underwood, Jeffrey Peach, William Long, Peter Lay).

IV. That the said Mr Newman read the booke granting liberty for sports & unlawfull recreations on the Lord's day. And hath stood & looked upon his parishioners whilst they have been playeing at footeball upon the saboth day to the great incourageing of his people therein. (Henry Underwood, Robert Nutt, Peter Lay).

V. That he never to their knowledge kept any day of thanksgivinge appointed by the Parlement, except the last which was kept by his Curate, upon the Saboth day. And suffreth but one sermon upon the fast dayes, whereby his famely and ill affected parishioners had liberty to goe about their worldly imployments or unlawfull recreations to the great dishonor of Almighty god without any reprooffe. (Richard Robinson, Robert Nutt, Henry Underwood, Jeffrey Peach, William Walters).

VI. That the said Mr Newman's servants made hay upon the day of thanks-giveinge appointed to be kept for london's deliverance. (William Walters).

VII. That he is a frequent haunter of Alehouses, and hath been misordered with over much drinke and is a swearer, espially when he is in beere. (Christopher Gibbons, James Raynham, Henry Underwood, Robert Nutt, William Walters, William Long, Jeffrey Peach, Peter Lay).

VIII. That the said Mr Newman, when the Associated armes were sent to Cambridge from Sudbury, was there drinking at the Crowne with one John Marshall, where Mr Newman & Marshall scuffled one with the other, and after they were parted Marshall called for one iugg more to fox the parson outright. (Peter Lay, William Long).

IX. That he invited divers of his neighbours to diner in a Christide time. After they eate & drunke sufficiently Mr Newman caused divers men & woemen to be thrust into his buttery, their owne husbands & wives being absent, and there locked them upp & conveyed away the key. (William and Susan Long).

X. That he being drinkinge at the Christofer att Sudbury endeavored to have foxed one Jeffrey Peach with tent wyne, but the said Mr Newman drunke so much as he was not able to go the direct way to his owne house but went neer one mile & halfe out of his way. (Jeffrey Peach).

XI. That the said Mr Newman came to Peter Lay in a disguised manner with beere where he was at plow after he had fox't one Thomas Holborow & Richard Rollingson, & would not be satisfied except Peter Lay would permitt him to hold the plow, the which he did, but being not able to follow the plow he fell upon his knees sayeing a pox & plague take the driver. After which Mr Newman would have the said Lay go into a house where he inveighed against the Parlement sayeing they raised money to pay Mr Pim's debts. (Peter Lay).

XII. That Mr Newman about the end of May last went through some parte of litle Cornard being disguised with beere, hallowinge & throweing up his hatt. (Peter Lay).

XIII. That Mr Newman for the most parte, when he goeth about his parish to gather his tithe cheeses, retorneth home drunke behaveinge himselfe like a wildman. (Robert Nutt, Henry Underwood, Peter Lay, Jeffrey Peach).

XIV. That he hath with some of his townesmen at his owne house upon the saboth dayes & upon other dayes drunke so hard that they have been well laden with beere. And he hath come home from other placs full of beer being therewith very merry. (No witnesses).

XV. That notwithstanding he is a good wrestler, yett being at an alehouse received a fall by one that wrestled with him at midnight. (William Walters).

XVI. That he never incouraged his parishioners to assist the Parlement by their persons or estates, neither hath he prayed for the prosperinge of the

Parliament's army that ever wee heard. (Robert Nutt, William Walters, Henry Underwood, Peter Lay, Jeffrey Peach, William Long).

XVII. That he did, when the first weekely assessment was to be collected, refuse to pay the same, sayeinge unto the Constable who demanded it that he would not parte with his money to maynteyne forcs raised against his Kinge. And also said the Parliament were rebells against the king, forasmuch as they tooke up armes against their Kinge. (Jeffrey Peach being constable. The latter part is also affirmed by Henry Tanner the younger).

XVIII. That Mr Newman said the Parliament & the whole kingdome ought to lay downe their neckes before the Kinge & submitt to performe whatsoever he should commaund them, or words to that effect. (Peter Lay, Jeffrey Peach).

XIX. That he said he knew the Kinge was in the right way, and he would never send out any armes untill the kinge & Parliament were agreed, neither would he pray for the Parliament so longe as he lived. (William Long).

XX. That his discourse oftentimes is full of bawdry not fitt to be repeated by modest & sober men; and hath been very uncivill both in speeches & actions towards his wife in the presence of his neighbours. (William Walters, Peter Lay, Jeffrey Peach).

XXI. That the said Mr Newman about 2 yeeres since, being in discourse in his owne house with one John Marshall & others about woemen's secrets, Mr Newman demanded of Marshall by what name he thought it was called. Marshall not answeringe, Mr Newman said that it was called a ——— [sic] and he would prove it, to which end he presently fetched a booke to shew the said Marshall that it was therin so called. (James Raynham).

Newman is married with 3 children; the living is worth £100 a year, and he has £100 a year personal estate.

1644 28th June: the witnesses set their hands to this, having testified the same upon oath.

Proved before:- Nathaniel Bacon, Nathaniel Bacon, Thomas Chaplin, Thomas Tirrell, Brampton Gurdon.

Newman was ejected on the 2nd September 1644, Manchester's warrant being directed to Henry Underwood, William Walters, Jeffrey Peach, Thomas Cooke.

Articles against William Pratt, Rector of Melton.

I. That the said Mr Pratt gave £100 for the said livinge (as himselfe confessed). (Robert Hallifax snr.).

II. That he was a constant observer of Bishopp Wren's iniunctions and superstitious inovations (vizt) bowinge towards the rayles & bowinge att the name of Jesus and all other. And hath often threatned to have the Churchwardens severely punished if they did not present, at the Ecclesiasticall Court, all such as did not observe the same Inovations. (John Chandler, Richard Clare, George Peake, John Nuttall, Robert Hallifax).

III. That he refused to administer the sacrament to one Thomas Cotton because he refused to come upp to the rayles to receyve the same, & so persecuted the said Cotton that no man might sett him on worke, harbour or have any society with him to the great greife & losse of the said Cotton. And also by threats he caused to be presented at the late Commissarye's Court one Robert Haughten & endeavored to have severall other persons likewise presented for not cominge upp to the rayles to receyve the sacrament. (Robert Hallifax, John Chandler, Richard Clare).

IV. That he threatned them that went to other Churches, though they went when there was no sermon at the said Church of Melton. (Robert Hallifax).

V. When the communion table, standinge under the East window where the crucifix stood, was according to command of Parliament removed, he comanded it to be sett there agayne. (Richard Clare).

VI. That he refused to read the bookes sent by order of parliament in the Church, but appointed another place, amongst which one was for raisinge of mony, horse & plate. And himselfe never lent to the propositions of parliament, only gave 40/– or £3 as they have been informed. (Mark Edmonds).

VII. That he refused to read the first vow and covenant, sayeinge, it did not concerne him and endeavored to discorage others from takinge it. (Robert Hallifax, Richard Clare).

VIII. That he seldom preacheth, & then read his sermons wholly. And he much sleighted & neglected the monethly fast, reading the booke sett out when the Scotts the first time came into England. ('All to this').

IX. That though he hath been parson there theis 33 yeeres & upwards, and hath gotten a good estate in lands & money, yet he suffers the Chancell, parsonage house, barnes, stables & other buildings to decay so that the necessary repayre thereof will cost £40 at least. (Robert Hallifax, John Chandler, Richard Clare).

Proved on the 2nd April 1644 before Nathaniel Bacon, Robert Brewster, Francis Brewster, Peter Fisher, Robert Duncon, John Base.

Manchester's warrant for the ejection of Pratt is undated and undirected.

Articles against Daniel Wicherley, Rector of Hemingstone and Fellow of Queens' College, Cambridge.[1]

[1] In 1705 Walker received an interesting assessment of Wicherley's character and the case against him from William Thorne, whose father had told him a good deal concerning the circumstances of the sequestration (Ms. J. Walker, c. 3, f. 191). Thorne's father had a high opinion of Wicherley, and when some of the parish requested him to join them in pressing Articles against the minister he refused 'upon the account of the Articles being false'. Thorne concluded his letter, 'In short, I knew the Gentleman myself & I never saw nor ever heard of any misdemeanour or fault sufficient to eject him out of his living, but his not being of their faction'.

However, the historical value of this testimonial is doubtful. Thorne states that Wicherley was accused on 16 Articles, and proceeds to quote three of them. In fact none appear in the charge against Wicherley, although two are accusations against Proctor (see below, pp. 89–90).

I. That the said Daniel Wicherley hath beene Rector of the said parish for the space of seven yeeres & upward, and hath never been resident there but hath placed unworthy Curats in his absence who were some of them very scandalous in their lives & conversations. (John Stiles gent., John Smith, Anthony Muskett).

II. That he seemed to us to be very malignant haveinge not paid his assessments both for the weekely pay & the 5th & 20th parte, which monyes could not be gotten but by distrayninge his parishioners for the same. (John Freborne, John Stiles, John Smith).

III. That whereas the nationall covenant was given by his Curat to some of the parishioners upon the 10th day of March last and notice was given that such as were not then there should have it tendered unto them upon another Lord's day and the said Mr Wicherley cominge to towne soon after, thereupon it was wholly neglected so as some that were not there the first day & are desirous to take it could never since have liberty to take it. And the said Mr Wicherley hath not to our knowledge taken the said covenant. (John Stiles, Lionel Curtis, John Smith, John Freborne).

IV. The said Mr Wicherley, when he hath been at his said cure, hath given a very bad example both by prophaninge of the Lord's day & usually makinge bargaynes for his tithes upon that day, and receivinge monyes & other disorders. (John Stiles, John Smith).

V. The said Mr Wicherley hath wholly neglected the supply of the cure divers fast dayes & many Lord's dayes so as wee have had none either to babtise our children or bury the dead. Insomuch that the dead corps hath stood all night in the church there being no minister to read at the buriall, nor the freinds of the deceased dared then to interre them without such readinge. (John Blye, Ann Colman, George Aldred).

VI. That the said Curat being now gonn and the said Mr Wicherley also is absent from us, so as wee are wholly destitute of preachinge, sacraments & divine worshipp in our Church. (John Stiles, John Smith, John Freborne).

VII. The said Mr Wicherley doth maynteyne that the Earle of Newcastle is as good a protestant as himself or any other in the university. (John and Elizabeth Stiles, John Freborne).

VIII. The said Mr Wicherley saith the Scotts are a trecherous kind of people and ever were, and that if they gett into our kingdom wee shall not gett rid of them againe, but they wilbe ready to cutt our throtes, for they come for no good. (John and Elizabeth Stiles, Ann Colman).

The 19th and the 23rd Articles). The third, which does not appear in the charges against any Suffolk minister, is amusing. 'He made his parishoners, when he went perambulation, drunk & then overreacht them in bargaining for their Tythes.' And Thorne adds to this that the Article 'was no truer (my father said) than the other two, for he said there was but one drunk then & that he would not be at rest till he had compounded with him; besides my father said, his parishoner was then very well satisfied with Mr Wicherly's demands & that his Tythes were a good pennyworth much more.'

But despite the wealth of circumstantial detail it would seem that Thorne's recollections of his father's comments concerning Wicherley were dimmed by the sixty-year time-lag.

IX. That the said Mr Wicherley saith he could not tell what to make of the first covenant it was such a blind devotion. (John and Elizabeth Stiles).

X. That the said Mr Wicherley being told of the badnes of his curate, his answer was wee must do as they say and not as they doe. (John Stiles, Ann Colman).

XI. The said Mr Wicherley when he hath beene at our cure hath used to bow towards the rayle or comunion table as he went & likewise to read second service at the comunion table. (John Talmage, John Stiles, John Blye).

The Living is worth £80 a year – but the parsonage house and barns are badly decayed.

13th May 1644 these Articles were proved before Nathaniel Bacon, William Bloys, Robert Duncon, Peter Fisher and John Base, and Mr Wicherley had warninge by a note left at the parsonage house & yett did not appeare.

Manchester's warrant for the ejection of Wicherley is neither dated nor directed.

Articles against William Aldus, Rector of Copdock; previously Curate of Blaxhall.

I. That the said William Aldus hath been superstitious in his practizes about the late inovations, boweing to the rayles or communion table in goeing upp & goeing downe to & from them. (Mark Secker,[1] Francis Crispe, Edward Gooles).

II. That he ordinarily read second service within the rayles at the Comunion table. (Francis Crispe, Edward Gooles, Mark Secker).

III. That in Bishopp Wren's tyme he would not administer the sacrament of the Lord's supper to any except they came upp to the rayles to receive the same. (Francis Crispe, Edward Gooles).

IV. That he is a common alehousehaunter & a frequenter of tavernes. (Robert Harvey, Francis Woodweigh, Richard Winter, Mark Secker, Edward Gooles).

V. That he hath been often drunke or distempered with excesse of beere & wyne. (Mark Secker, Robert Harvey, Richard Winter).

VI. That at the buriall of Everard Goules his sister he was so distempered with excesse of beere or wyne that he could not read the buriall. (Richard Taylor, John Deane).

VII. That at the buriall of one George Lucas he was so distempered with excesse of beere or wyne that he could not performe any office of a minister, no, not read the Lord's prayer aright. (George Lucas, Mark Secker).

VIII. That he the said William Aldus was desired to bury one Jeffry Blanch-flower's child, and he told them that they should be ready by two of the

[1] All of these witnesses were from Blaxhall.

clocke and they did bringe it accordinge and staid untill 4 or 5 of the clocke, but he came not, neither that night nor the next morne but left it unburyed. (Mark Secker, Jeffrey Blanchflower).

IX. That the corps of one Mary Large being brought to the Churchgate and they not daring to carry it into the holy ground untill the Minister came, staid there 3 houres, and his wife sent from place to place to find him and at the last he came but was so distempered with beer as he was unfitt for any dutye. (Robert Large, Mark Secker).

X. That he spake against & reproched such as went to heare other Ministers for the good of their soules, sayeinge to Richard Secker, a yonge man that used to go to heare other Ministers, he would have him whipped if he did not leave his gaddinge. (Mark Secker, Francis Woodweigh).

Jonathan Basse, who was a grandJuryman at Woodbridge att the same time when complaint was made against him, beleiveth that he was indicted at the quarter Sessions at Woodbridge for a common drunkerd: Edward Gooles and Francis Crispe affirme that they heard of such a business against him.

Proved before Nathaniel Bacon, William Bloys, Peter Fisher, Robert Duncon, John Base, on the 30th April 1644.

Additional Articles against William Aldus.

I. That the said William Aldus upon the Lord's daye, being the 12th day of this instant May, in the parish Church of Cobdocke in the forenoone did publickly read the confession, absolution & other part of the service in the booke called the service booke. (Nathaniel Ralfe, Robert Hitchcock).

II. That about tuesday night being the last day of Aprill last past, he the said William Aldus, with one Edward Gooles came to a Taphouse in Eyke at the widow Prettyes, and there were tiplinge and drinking all or the most parte of that night and the next day till nyne or ten of the clock at night till his companion, Edward Gooles, was drunke. (William Bacon, William Chaplin).

III. That about 4 or 5 yeeres since a child being dead and he the said William Aldus being required to bury it, he willed it to be brought by 8 of the clocke in the morninge which they did, but before he was gone to Wickham and there was drinkinge & tiplinge 2 or 3 dayes & came not home untill his wife sent for him. (Robert Taylor).

IV. That the said William Aldus being procured to Glemham in the foreparte of the Lord's day, came home to Bloxhall in the afternoone and catechisinge the youth he said to the Churchwardens that one did disturbe him, and then pluckt of his hood & surplice and said there is an hundred marke lost & putt on his hatt & went away, leavinge all the people without publiq dutyes, no man knowinge any that disturbed him. (Robert Taylor).

Proved on the 13th May 1644 before Nathaniel Bacon, William Bloys, Peter Fisher, Robert Duncon, John Base.

Manchester's warrant for the ejection of Aldus is undated and undirected.

Articles against John Utting, Vicar of Corton; presented to the Committee sitting at Yoxford on the 20th June 1644.

I. That he is a notorious drunkerd, and upon Easter last was a yeere was so drunke the day before that the next day he could not administer the sacrament to them. And Francis Greene testifieth that in December last upon a saturday he was drinking most parte of the day and almost all that night, that the cure was neglected all that Lord's day. (Dennis Blanchflower, Anthony Winston, Francis Greene).

II. That he hath been indicted att the Assizes att Suffolk for incontinency & drunkennes and found guilty by the Grand Jury. (Thomas Ellis).

III. They exhibit a booke of Articles heere unto us which were proved upon oath by vertue of a Commission out of the Bishopp's Court att Norwich concerninge his incontinencye, drunkennes and other misdemeanors to which they all referr themselves, and the sentence hereuppon, which sentence never yett was executed.

1644 20th June: Proved before Nathaniel Bacon, Nathaniel Bacon, Robert Brewster, Francis Brewster, Peter Fisher, John Base.

Mr. Uttinge had day given him to the 8th of Julye to bring in his defence, but brought none.

Manchester's warrant ejecting Utting is undated and undirected.

Articles against Robert Sugden, Vicar of Benhall.

I. That the said Mr Robert Sugden is a common ale-house haunter and a companion of alehouse haunters, and a notorious drunkerd continueinge tiplinge at the ale-house aswell night as dayes in a very beastly manner. (Robert Hayward, Richard Crow).

II. The said Mr Sugden hath been vehemently suspected for incontinency with severall woemen, but especially with one Anne Shepherd a singlewoman who hath had a bastard. (Robert Felgat, Robert Hayward).

III. The said Mr Sugden hath been very forward to observe the late Innovations in frequent bowinge at the name of Jesus, even since the ordinance of Parliament forbidding the same; and caused the comunion table to be tourned alter wise and to be sett att the upper end of the chancell under the east window and comonly bowed towards the said table both when he went to it & when he came from it, and caused a forme to be sett before the said table (being sett alterwise) before the raile was made, that the people might kneele at the said forme; and caused one, old Smith, a lame man, to creepe upon his hand out of the body of the Church into the chancell, and two antient woemen, the one very old & the other blind to be taken out of their seats & lead upp into the Chancell or elce he would not deliver them the communion; and hath turned backe some from the comunion for no other cause but that they would not come upp [*and*] kneele before the raile. (Thomas Grimsby, Francis Newson, Brian Hatton, ? Ellis, Stephen Hatton, Robert Hayward, Robert Felgat).

IV. The said Mr Sugden did publickly on the Lord's day read the booke of sports for profaninge the said day. (Robert Hayward, Thomas Grimsby, and others).

V. The said Mr Sugden caused the wife of Goodman Turner to come upp to the raile when he was to give thanks for her safe delivery from Childbirth & commanded her to putt off her hat, upon which she was much troubled & presently after she sickned & dyed. (Robert Felgat, Francis Newson, William Crumpe).

VI. The said Mr Sugden refused to sett his hand to a petition for the removinge the popish Lords & Bishops out of the Parliament, sayeing it came from a pack of puritans, and said if he had it he would rend it in peics & burne it. (Austin Browne, Edward Reeve, John White [Wright?], Robert Hayward).

VII. The said Mr Sugden refused to take the first vow & covenant himselfe or to tender it to his parishioners. (Thomas Grimsby, Robert Felgat).

VIII. The said Mr Sugden hath been often absent from his cure and hath left the same often destitute without any to supply the same and when he hath putt in any he hath putt in none but such as have been scandalous in life or doctrine or both (vizt) Mr Sumpter, Mr Kinge, Mr Fenn, Mr Brunderey, Mr Goodinge, Mr Brawton[1] all theis with others that are now outed. (John White, Thomas Grimsby).

IX. The said Mr Sugden tooke the protestation with reservation that the Church might be governd by Bishopps, which caused some in his parish to take it with the same reservation. (John Grose, Robert Hayward).

X. When some of his parish have gone abroad to heare a godly minister preach the said Mr Sugden said they were ready to heare one pray blasphemy & preach treason. (Edward Reeve, Thomas Grimsby).

Mr Sugden had a note left at his house for his appearance before the Committee at Ipswich the 14th of Aprill 1644 to appeare the 16th of Aprill following, by me Thomas Grimsby.

16th April 1644 proved before Nathaniel Bacon, William Bloys, Francis Brewster, Robert Duncon, Peter Fisher, John Base.

There was day given to the said Mr Sugden to putt in his defence to theis Articles till the 30th day of Aprill & notice given to him accordingly by Robert Hayward one of the parishioners; and further day was also given till May 13th on which day the said Mr Sugden did not putt in his defence and made the like default on monday the 27th day of this instant May.

Thomas Tirrell, Nathaniel Bacon, William Bloys, Peter Fisher, Robert Duncon.

Manchester's warrant ejecting Sugden is undated and undirected.

[1] These ministers are Simon Sumpter, Rector of Badingham and Vicar of Ubbeston; Nicholas King, Vicar of Friston and Snape; William Fenn, Rector of Theberton; Hugh Brandereth, Rector of Swefling; Thomas Broughton, Rector of Chillesford. 'Mr Goodinge' is probably Nathaniel Goodwyn, who was sequestered from the vicarage of Cransford, a living about five miles from Benhall. See Matthews, pp. 329, 333, 336, 338, 345.

Articles against Nicholas Stoneham, Rector of Eyke; taken before the Committee sitting at Ipswich on the 15th April 1644.

I. That Mr Nicholas Stonham did use at the consecrating of the wyne in the sacrament to elevate or lift upp the wyne. (Laurence Spring, Robert Girling, Robert Alegood, John Stud).

II. That he did refuse to administer the sacrament to such as would not come upp to the rayles. (Laurence Spring, Robert Girling, Robert Alegood, John Stud, William Bugg).

III. That he affirmed that the place within the rayles was a sanctified place & that he would not come out. (John Stud, Laurence Spring, William Bugg, Robert Alegood, Robert Girling).

IV. That he is a common alehouse & tavern haunter. (Laurence Spring, John Robertson, Thomas Norman, Thomas Pope, Robert Alegood).

V. That he is a common swearer by the name of god, and other othes. (William Chaplin, Robert Alegood, John Robertson, William Yorke).

VI. That he hath been present with such of his parish as have been at the same tyme camping[1] on the Lord's day, & shewed no dislike thereof. (Laurence Spring, Thomas Pope, Robert Alegood).

VII. That he called the Parliament robbers of the country, and that the king might proclaime them theeves. (Robert Alegood, William Yorke).

VIII. That he neglecteth fasts, [*and*] abuseth them with workinge his horse & servants, himself pitchinge the cart. (Robert Alegood, William Yorke, Thomas Pope, John Robertson, William Chaplin).

IX. That as touchinge the Parliament he said if some of them did not gett them to their leggs their neckes might feele the weight of their bodyes. (Thomas Pope, William Chaplin).

The parsonage is valued at £50 per annum; Stoneham has £5 a year in personal estate, and has a wife and one child.

Proved before Nathaniel Bacon, Thomas Tirrell, William Bloys, Peter Fisher, Robert Duncon.

Manchester's warrant ejecting Stoneham is undated and undirected.

Articles against William Gibbons, Rector of Great and Little Bealings.

I. That the said Mr Gibbons hath been & is still a hanter of alehouses & taphouses, & hath been often distempered with excesse of beer & wyne. And Samuel Duncon testifies that he being a Constable in Ipswich carryed him before the Bayliffs of Ipswich where he paid 5/- for being drunke. (John Cockson, Richard Stephens).

II. That he is commonly reputed an Incontinent person, & a companion of lewd & incontinent woemen & a common drunkerd. (John Cockson, Richard Stephens, Jonathan Basse, Samuel Duncon).

---

[1] Camping was the traditional local ball-game: see *Victoria County History, Suffolk*, II, p. 384. From the Old English word meaning to contend.

III. That Mr Gibbons was taken by the watch about 10 of the clocke in the night in a private roome with two woemen noted to be harlotts. Jonathan Basse saw him in the same house with those woemen presently after being abroad that night with the watch. (John Cockson).

IV. That he in a suspitious & lustfull manner putt his hands under the clothes of Susan Scott, a noted harlott, att another tyme. (John Cockson).

V. That he was att another tyme in Woodbridge shutt upp in a private roome with another man's wife much suspected, (whose husband, as the fame goeth, he had sent out into the towne to buy reed heringes) and did in a shamefull & imodest manner draw forth his privy members. William Smart testifieth that in the same roome he saw them very merry togeither a litle before. (Richard Hayward, James Fryer).

1644 30th April: proved before Nathaniel Bacon, William Bloys, Peter Fisher, John Base, Robert Duncon.

Manchester's warrant ejecting Gibbons is undated and undirected.

Articles against John Ferror, Rector of Trimley St. Mary

I. That the said Ferrour is a conformist to popish & superstitious Innovations enioyned by Bishopp Wrenn. He hath caused the communion table to be sett upp alter wise; did his devotion, bowinge 3 tymes att every tyme he came before the rayles where they stood, and bowed towards the east & at the name of Jesus. (John King,*[1] Francis Woodroffe, Abigail Bennett, John Stebbing, James Bennett).

II. The said Ferrour caused the ten commandements to be sett upp at the east end of the chancell and caused them to be razed out on the north side of the church where they were fairly written. (John Bennett, John Gayford,* John King*).

III. The said Ferrour hath refused to give to a poor widow the sacrament of the lord's supper because shee refused to kneele at the rayles; she offred herselfe in the Chancell, yett he caused the Churchwardens to present her for not receivinge. (John King,* Francis Woodroffe, John Gayford,* John Bennett).

IV. The said Ferrour hath reproved for standing upp & not kneelinge whiles he read the letany or collects some of his parishioners; [also] others for putting on their hatts in the Church after publicke excercise was ended. (John King,* Abigail Bennett, John Gayford*).

V. The said Ferrour hath publickly tollerated the prophanation of the Lord's day by suffringe his house-hold servants to use pastime thereon and by sending his man oftentimes to the taverne at Walton for bottles of wyne in the afternoon on the lord's day. (Richard Merchant, William Betts, John Stebbing).

[1] An asterisk against the name of a witness signifies that he also testified against John Beadle, Rector of Trimley St Martin (see above, p. 48).

VI. The said Ferrour hath alwayes been very averse to the wholsome con-stitutions of parliament, sayeing their ordinancs were illegall. He hath refused to associate or lend upon the propositions untill he was enforced by imprisonement, whereby he did disherten others. (Samuel Courtnall,* William Blackman,* John Hart*, William Betts).

VII. The said Ferrour had theis severall passags in a sermon which he preached on the saboath next after the Constable received the first warrant for the weekely assessement; he said that the foule disease was by us called Morbus gallicus, by the french morbus Italicus, theft is now a dayes termed borrowing from such as are not willinge to lend. How that our king was wrongfully abused and called a man of bloud as David was by Shimei. He said that I (meaninge himselfe) should be forced to lend my money to maynteine a way tending to bloudshed. (William Ide, William Betts).

VIII. The said Ferrour hath utterly refused to take either of the two Cove-nants or to give it to his parishioners, whereby they be destitute of the protection of the Parliament through his aversenes. (John King,* William Ide, Nicholas Betts, John Harris).

1644 15th April: proved before Nathaniel Bacon, Peter Fisher, Nathaniel Bacon, Robert Duncon, William Bloys, Francis Brewster.

No answer brought in, though warned 2 monethes.

Manchester's warrant ejecting Ferror is undated and undirected.

Articles against Edward Barton, Rector of Grundisburgh.

I. That the said Mr Barton hath not continued att his livinge since he came to be a parson of that parish, but hath heretofore come thither once or twice in a yeere for a weeke or a fortnight to receive the proffitts of the livinge.

II. That the said Mr Barton hath wholly absented himselfe from his livinge by the space of one yeer and 3 quarters last past, notwithstanding the parliament have declared their dislike of such as are non resident.

III. That the said Mr Barton hath an infirme body & noe audible voice.

IV. That the said Mr Barton doth constantly read his sermons which he performes very imperfectly and doth not usually exceed the space of half an houre.

V. That the said Mr Barton hath not come to the towne nor sent any Curate, although his former Curate did forsake the place about a quarter of a yeere since, so that the parish hath been wholly destitute divers Lord's dayes. (Hundon Hart, Edward Black, George Lard, Richard Hill – to all the articles).

1644 1st April: Proved before Nathaniel Bacon of Friston, Robert Brewster, William Bloys, Francis Bacon, John Base, Thomas Tirrell, Peter Fisher.

Manchester issued the warrant for the ejection of Barton on the 7th August, 1644; it was directed to William Bloys, Esq., alone.

Articles against William Franklin, Rector of Flowton.

I. That the said Mr Franklyn was a constant observer of Bishopp Wren's Iniunctions, bowinge att & toward the Rayles in ascending & descending to & from the same, and also boweing at the name of Jesus. (William Tillett, George Gardner, Thomas Manninge, Thomas Hall, William Goodall).

II. That he threatned and did publikely chide those that would not bow at the name of Jesus and observe the late Bishopp's orders. (Thomas Hall, William Goodall).

III. That he denyed to administer the sacrament to such as would not come upp to the rayles to receive the same, & especially William Tillett who was excomunicate for not cominge upp to the rayles to receive the sacrament. And the said Tillet, at the said Mr Franklyn's instance was putt forceably out of the Church before the said excomunication was pronounced. (William Tillett, George Gardner).

IV. That the table being brought downe into the usuall place & bread & wyne being provided, he refused to administer the sacrament. (George Gardner, William Goodall).

V. That he is a common alehouse haunter & frequenter of tavernes, and often he hath been distempered with excesse of beere or wyne so that he could neither goe nor stand. (William Condycote, Howell Wright, Thomas Hall).

VI. That upon a sonday morning as the watchmen att Neadham retorned homeward they found the said Mr Francklyn laid in the high way distempered with excesse of beere or wyne, and nor farr from him a man & a woman, both scandalous persons. (John Parker, William Simpson).

VII. That he hath been frequent in alehouses & twice distempered with excesse of wyne & beere att Hadley. (Martin Norris).

VIII. That in the night tyme about 12 of the clocke, being accompanied with two scandalous whores, the said Mr Franklyn used abusive & railing speeches against the watchmen at Somersham who desired the said Mr Franklyn to go home & leave that company. And after that they found him in the standinge corn, the woemen running away, as the watchmen coniectured. (Francis Cole, John Damont).

IX. That he is a companion of scandalous woemen and hath been often in company with such in alehouses & suspicious houses & at unseasonable houres and hath been very uncivill in their company, his cariage being such towards them as is a shame to speake off. (William Tillett, George Gardner, Howell Wright, John Damont, William Goodall).

X. That he never preached on the fast dayes to our knowledge. (Thomas Webb, George Gardner).

XI. That he hath been very negligent in officiating the said cure, being often absent [*and*] never preachinge twice a day. (George Gardner, Thomas Hall).

XII. That he caused to be presented at the Ecclesiasticall Court William Tillett & Judeth Mannynge and others for goeing to other Churches though

at such tymes as when there was no sermon at their owne parish Church.
(William Tillett, William Goodall).

1644 15th April: proved before William Bloys, Nathaniel Bacon, Robert
Duncon, Francis Brewster, Peter Fisher.

*Manchester's warrant for the ejection of Franklin is undated and
undirected.*

*Articles against Thomas Sayer, Vicar of Hoxne, examined by the Com-
mittee sitting at Diss on the 7th June 1644.*

I. Inprimis Hillary Fermor & George Norfew of Hoxne aforesaid do say
upon their oathes that the said Mr Thomas Sayer hath been vicar of the
towne of Hoxne for the space of about eight & forty yeeres.

II. Item John Newman & Nicholas Goslinge of Hoxne aforesaid do say upon
their oathes that the said Mr Sayer hath for theis many yeeres last past very
seldom preached himself, but for the most parte hath sett those to supply
his place as are & have been very superstitious or exceedinge scandalous &
ill affected persons, to the great greife & offence of the well affected Christians
in his parish.

III. Item Samuel Huntinge of Hoxne aforesaid & the said Nicholas Goslinge
do say upon their oathes that the said Mr Sayer hath presented or caused to
be presented & excommunicated many of his parishioners in the Ecclesiasticall Court for not comming to their parish Church when they have gonne
to heare other godly Ministers.

IV. Item Ursula Coleman of Eye & Nicholas Selfe of Hoxne aforesaid do
say upon their oathes that the said Mr Sayer commonly useth playeinge att
Cards with his familye, sometymes with his servants & sometymes with
others.

V. Item the said John Newman & Hillary Fermor do say upon their oathes
that the said Mr Sayer, when he used to preach while Bishopp Wren was
Bishopp of Norwich, did not only practise but frequently pressed & preached
for the said Bishopp's innovated Iniunctions; & in his preaching hath taught
that there was no superstition in the Bishopp's order & iniunctions, and
they were all fooles that said there was, useing many words to that purpose
or effect.

VI. Item Samuel Bullen & Henry Roper of Hoxne aforesaid do say upon
their oathes that the said Mr Sayer did preach for Bishop Wren's superstitious Iniunctions, and att one tyme in his pulpett used theis or the like
words, Some make a scruple to go up to the rayles forsooth and to kneele
there forsooth, but they had better go thither then go a further iourney,
meaninge to the Court as theis deponents verily conceived.

VII. Item the said Henry Roper & John Goslinge of Hoxne aforesaid do say
upon their oathes that he forced divers of his parish to receyve the sacrament when they were to be marryed and refused otherwise to marry them.

VIII. Item the said John Newman & William Wilby of Okeley do say upon their oathes that the said Mr Sayer hath suffered vayne sports upon the Lord's dayes, and frequent shooting & camping neere his house; and there hath been great shootinge and he never reproved any for the same that any of us do know or have heard of.

IX. Item Thomas Dye of Hoxne aforesaid gent., & the said George Morfew do say upon their oathes that the said Mr Sayer caused the said Thomas Deye, sometime Churchwarden of the towne of Hoxne, to be sued in two Ecclesiasticall Courts for sayeing he would raise no high Alters in the Chancell. Oftentimes he urged the said Mr Dey to sett up the said rayle, and because he would not he caused him to be accused thereof to Bishopp Wrenn, whereby he was continually molested untill about the tyme the Parliament first satt.

X. Item Priscilla Clarke, widow, of Hoxne aforesaid doth say upon her oath that she went to the said Mr Sayer & desired the sacrament from the rayle in some seat in the Church or att some privat house; she told him that if she went to the rayle she went against her conscience. He told her that her conscience was erronious, and if she would not come to the rayle he would not give it her, but would make her an example to the whole towne. . . . The next day he refused to give [her] the sacrament & putt her into the Court.

XI. Item the said John Goslinge doth say upon his oath that the said Mr Sayer incouraged him, the said John who served in his armes,[1] to go fight against the Scotts, telling him that if he dyed in that warre he should dye a Martyr, with some other encoraging words.

XII. Item William Huntinge of Frandeston[2] doth say upon his oath that there hath been many tymes shooting & other sports used by the yonge persons in Hoxne upon the lord's dayes, and about a yeere since this deponent did see the said Mr Sayer lookinge towards his parishioners while they were shootinge at the butts upon the lord's day.

XIII. Item Symon Rush of Hoxne aforesaid and the said Samuel Bullen do say upon their oathes that the said Mr Sayer hath preached but once or twice in a quarter of a yeere now last past in his said parish Church.

XIV. Item Alexander Chilver & Mary Selfe of Hoxne aforesaid do say upon their oathes that the said Mr Sayer seldom preacheth on the fast dayes, and in Harvest last gave liberty to his parishioners to worke in the afternoone.

XV. Item the said Hillary Fermour doth say that the said Mr Sayer hath a wife & foure children all married, or have been marryed & about £10 per annum besides the £40 he hath by his wife.

Proved before Tobias Frere, John Greenwood, Henry Kinge, Robert Gooch, Thomas Lincoln.

Manchester's warrant for the ejection of Sayer is dated the 8th July 1644, and is directed to Hillary Fermour, Samuel Bullen, George Pulman junior and Samuel Hunting.

[1] Gosling would have attended the musters of the local trained-band at the expense of, and in equipment provided by, Sayer.

[2] i.e. Thrandeston.

Articles against Thomas Ambler, Vicar of Wenhaston, examined on the 20th June 1644 by the Committee sitting at Yoxford.

I. The said Mr Ambler doth comonly sweare by his faith. (John Poynting).

II. The said Mr Ambler is a frequenter of alehouses as namely to the house of Edmond Browne & divers other placs; and [*is*] a Companion of drunkerds & disordered malignant persons. (Thomas Greene, John Poynting).

III. He is an enemy to the Parliament and doth give out reprochfull speeches concerning the proceedinges of the Parliament; as namely the Parliament goes about to pick every penny of money out of your purses. And he being demanded the assessment of the 5th & 20th parte by the Constable he answered that it is high treason to pay it: who dare troope me for the same, I will not pay it. (John Poynting, Thomas Green).

IV. He refused to take the first covenant & published to the people of the said towne that it was a dangerous oath & I wish you to beware of it, and they that had taken the same were all periured & would be hanged. (John Poynting).

Thomas Greene addeth further that he did not take it neither would he publish it, sayeing it came not with authority enough.

V. He hath defended the booke of sports upon the lord's day and some persons that desired his assistance towards the suppressinge of sports upon that day he told them they had nothing to do with it, there was a booke of liberty. And hath sent to the mill for ground malt upon the lord's day, & suffred yong people to campe[1] before his house upon the lord's day. (Richard Aldred, Thomas Hassell).

VI. He hath affirmed in his preachinge that forgivenes of sins belonge not to god onelye, vouchinge the booke of comon prayer for it, and in an alehouse he affirmed he himselfe could forgive sins; and he hath in his preaching affirmed that there are seaven petitions in the lord's prayer. (John Poynting, Richard Aldred, Robert Ludbrooke, John Pace.)

VII. He hath been conformable to all Bishop Wrenne's Iniunctions, as namely to bow before the communion table and at the mentioning of the name of Jesus, and to preach in his surplice, and did not pray before his sermon but according to the Bishopp's Iniunctions, and doth yett stand upp at Gloria patri. (John Poynting, Richard Aldred, Thomas Hassell).

VIII. He hath refused to deliver the sacrament of the lord's supper in any other place but at the rayles. (John Poynting, Richard Aldred).

IX. He hath published in the Church at Wenhasted the King's proclamation whereby he manifest the great successe his Majesty had had & his victoryes. (Thomas Aldred, John Fiske).

The living is worth £25 per annum, and Ambler has a wife and 4 children.

Proved before: Nathaniel Bacon, Nathaniel Bacon, Robert Brewster, Francis Brewster, Peter Fisher, John Base.

Manchester's warrant for the ejection of Ambler, which is undirected, is dated the 24th June 1644.

[1] See note on p. 70 above, and cf. article VIII on p. 75.

Articles against Seth Chapman, Rector of Hasketon.

I. The said Seth Chapman hath been a great & forward observer of the late Innovations, vizt. a constant goer upp unto the alter to read second service. (Thomas Tym, Richard Sewett, Robert Collington).

II. That as he went upp & as he came away he crouched & bowed often superstitiously. (Thomas Tym, Richard Sewett, Robert Collington, Nathaniel Atherall).

III. That when he baptised any children he would compell the godfathers & godmothers to kneele downe at the font; and laid his hands upon one Thomas Draper to pull him downe upon his knees because he refused to kneele and would have turned him out of the Church because he would not kneele. (Thomas Tym, Thomas Draper, William Finch, Richard Sewett).

IV. That when he churched woemen he compelled them to come up to the alter & caused them to kneele & so he churched them there. (Thomas Tym, Richard Sewett, Nathaniel Atherall).

V. That at the buriall of the dead he caused the people to kneele upon the ground duringe most parte of the buriall. (George Mann, Thomas Tym, William Finch).

VI. That he is evill affected to king & parliament, for he is hardly drawne to publish ordinancs of Parliament or when he doth publish any he never stirrs upp the people by any word of exhortation. (John Goose, Thomas Huggen).

VII. That when the first covenant was to be taken, the lord's day next after the receivinge of it he snebbed John Goose because he was forward in it & went presently away so that that day none but the said John Goode, his sonn & man would take the said covenant. (John Goose, Thomas Goodale, Thomas Huggen, William Finch).

VIII. That the said Seth Chapman would not take the said covenant according to the ordinance, but did take his owne covenant after this manner (vizt.), Savinge my former oathes, vowes, protestations & promises & so farr as lawfully I may, I, Seth Chapman do take this vow & covenant. And by his example the most parte of the parish tooke it with the same reservation that he the said Seth Chapman tooke. And [he] still keeps it from the Churchwarden so that they that did not take it cannot be retorned according to the ordinance. (Thomas Goodale, Thomas Huggen, William Finch).

IX. That when John Goose delivered to him the said Seth Chapman an ordinance for the Lord Fairfax & desired him to stirr upp the people to a free lendinge or contribution he fell to railinge aginst Thomas Huggen & him, the said John Goose, calling the parishioners to beare witnes that if his wife or child died within a yeere & a day that he laid their bloud to the charge of the said Thomas Huggen & John Goose, & so made a disturbance that hindred the contribution. (Nathaniel Atherall, John Goose, Thomas Goodale, William Finch).

X. That he preacheth but once on the lord's day till within this moneth, nor but once on the fast day, whereby much profannes & wickednes was donn on those days (vizt), working on the fast dayes, wrastling, drinking, & ringing both on fast & lord's dayes, and he used no meanes to hinder it. (Nathaniel Atherall, John Goose, Thomas Goodale, William Finch).

XI. That he in severall sermons told the people that if they did not confesse all their sins to the minster of their parish or to some other learned devine that their soules could not be saved as he stedfastly beleeved, and that there was none of us upon our sickbedds but would be glad to receive the comfort of the keyes. (Thomas Tym, Richard Sewett, Robert Collington).

XII. That he being sent for to come to visitt an honest man of his parish in the tyme of his sicknes, did come to him accordingly and after the sick man had recovered his health he & his wife mett with the said Seth Chapman, preist, who amonge other words told the man that in the time of his sicknes he could have used such rash speeches unto him as would have frighted him and sent him to hell. (Thomas and Mary Huggen).

XIII. That he caused a peice of glasse painted to be removed from the south window in the Chancell, to the likenes of Christ nailed upon the Crosse, to be sett & placed in the East window of the Chantell over the alter there, & said that it was fittinge it should stand there to putt playne people in remembrance of Christ; & that he himselfe did idolize it in boweinge reverence. (Thomas Tym, George Man, William Finch).

XIV. That when the said Seth Chapman did come into the Chancell he alwayes kneeled downe upon his knees with his face towards the picture and held upp his hands towards it as though he had worshipped it. (Thomas Tym, George Mann).

XV. That when he, the said Seth Chapman, administred the sacrament of the lord's supper he in a superstitious way elevated the bread & wyne. (William Cracknell, Thomas Tym).

XVI. That he still useth to read the absolution and other humane traditions in the worshipp of God not warranted by the word of God, nor used by the best reformed Churches, notwithstanding his taking the late covenant. (John Goose, Thomas Huggen).

XVII. That for the space of three yeeres he never observed the fifth of November appointed by act of Parliament, but absented himselfe and caused his man to worke on that day. (Thomas Tym, Richard Sewett, Robert Collington).

XVIII. That when the Earle of Strafford was upon his triall the said Seth Chapman said that there is but one wise man in the kingdome and they goe about to take away his life. (Thomas Tym).

XIX. That he, the said Seth Chapman, hath donne much wast upon the gleabe cuttinge downe bodyes of bearinge poylings and hath sold some of them. (William Cracknell, Nathaniel Atherall).

1644 16th April: Proved before Peter Fisher, William Bloys, Robert Duncon, Nathaniel Bacon, John Base.

Manchester's warrant for the ejection of Chapman is undated and undirected.

Articles against Lionel Playters, Rector of Uggeshall, examined by the Committee sitting at the sign of the Griffen, Yoxford, on the 20th June 1644.[1]

I. The said Lionell Playters hath conformed himselfe to all Bishop Wren's Iniunctions and used constantly to preach in his surplice, to bow at the name of Jesus, and frequently at his entrance into the chancell and at his goeing up to the rayles he hath made much obeysance and many leggs & cringings before the comunion table & rayles. (Thomas Crowfoot, Nicholas Anderson, Edward Gilde).

II. He hath published in his Church the booke of sports upon the Lord's day and spake much in comendation of the same to encourage people to the observation thereof. (Francis Morse, Thomas Crowfoot).

III. When, according to an ordinance of Parliament, the Churchwardens had pulled up the rayles he gave out some threatninge speeches against them, and required them to have them forthcominge at their perills. (John Foxley, William Ellis).

IV. It doth not appeare that he hath associated nor taken the first covenant, but when that covenant was delivered unto him he said it did not belonge unto him, and lett them looke to it whom it did concerne. (Nicholas Anderson, William Crawfoot, Thomas Wallin).

V. In his preaching the said Lionell Playters hath uttered scandalous words against the Parliament & their proceedings in theis words or to this purpose (Thomas Crowfoot), namely:

a) that all those that exercise the Militia, muster or take upp armes, or call any men togeither, or beare or send in any armes, without the King's Comission shall receyve to themselves damnation. (Nicholas Anderson).

[1] Lionel Playters was the younger brother of Sir William Playters, Bart., of Sotterley, who was M.P. for Orford in the Long Parliament, and who remained, with some reluctance, in the Parliamentary camp during the war (see my thesis, op. cit., pp. 73–4). On the death of Sir William and of his son, a Royalist commander during the war, Lionel Playters succeeded to the baronetcy. From his son, Sir John, Walker received an interesting account of Lionel's troubles during the war (Ms. J. Walker, c. 1, f. 271). These began early in 1643 when his stable was raided; when Playters asked by what authority those involved acted they replied 'pistoll the parson' and fired 2 shots at him. Later Playters's opponents tore up brasses and the altar rails in the Church, and levelled the chancell, finding and keeping 200 gold pieces which Playters had buried in a grave for safety. Sir John also gives an account of events after the above Articles had been exhibited to the Committee at Yoxford. He states that his father made several Answers to the Articles, but that these were disregarded and he was sequestered. Manchester's warrant ordering the sequestration was served on Playters on the 24th July by Thomas Crowfoot, Nicholas Anderson and William Ellis, who refused to allow him any time to find his family alternative accommodation; a few days later they entered his lands and seized his crops, which they converted to their own use. The sequestrators never returned any account of the profits of the rectory before 1646, allowed several buildings to collapse, and never paid Playters's wife her fifth part. The minister's difficulties did not end there, however; at the time of his prosecution his tenants were ordered to retain the rents they owed to their landlord for the hire of his personal estate, and in the resultant confusion many farms were left untenanted. As a result Playters received no rent for two years, but was still forced to pay Parliamentary taxes on the untenanted land.

b) that whatsoever forcs are or hath been otherwise raised are & mustbe against the king's person, and that no cause will tollerate resistance, neither was it lawfull to take upp armes for offence or defence without the Kinge's commission, and none could plead necessity in taking upp of armes, and that such as have or shall take upp armes without the king's Commission receyve to themselves damnation. (William Crawfoot, Edward Gilde).

c) That although David was anointed before he tooke away the speere & the cruse from King Saul, yett he restored them to him agayne; but who restores our king the speere & the sheild, the tower or the shipps, his townes, castles, guns, tribut, customes, or composition which are taken from him? Nay, they are so farr from restoring them that they employ them against him.

d) that a kinge was not to be resisted in any cause, although he should be a tirant; and that as wilfulnes made the 250 princs to rebell against Moses, so likewise pride & willfulnes is the cause of this rebellion amongst us. (John Foxley).

VI. The said Lionel Playters in his preaching hath spoken high in comendation of the Church of Rome and very contemptuously of the Church of England, extolling them for their greate preferrements of their Clergy before ours. (Thomas Crowfoot, Nicholas Anderson, John Foxley).

VII. He hath absented himselfe from the Justice of the Parliament by the space of 3 weekes or a moneth, & refused to pay the two payes of the great subsidyes untill he was distrayned for them. (Thomas Crowfoot, Nicholas Anderson, Edward Gilde).

VIII. Upon the last day of August 1642, being one of the fast dayes appointed by this honourable Parliament, he did wholly neglect to observe the said day as is commanded, and was part of the said day at the house of one Thomas Pightlin, drinking with one (   ) [sic] Patrick, a papist & an Armorer, which Armorer (as it is reported) is since gonn to the Cavaleers & popish Army. (Prudence Pightlin, Anne Callendar).

IX. Also the said Lyonel Playters, about the beginning of January last, said that he had hempe to sell & he hoped to sell it well for if theis tymes hold many would need hanging. (Susan Fair Ellis).
And he did further affirme that he had tenne stone of hempe & he would bestow it freely to hang up the Roundheads. (John George).

X. And further the said Lionel Playters, upon spillinge of the salt, said save the salt for salt wilbe deare; and the reason was asked him and he made answer the Roundheads must be salted. (John George, Susan Fair Ellis).

The Parsonage is worth £60 per annum, and his own property is valued at £200 per annum; he has a wife and four children.

Proved before Nathaniel Bacon, Nathaniel Bacon, Peter Fisher, Robert Brewster, Francis Brewster, John Base.

Manchester's warrant for the ejection of Playters is undated and undirected. (But see note 1, page 79.)

Articles against Thomas Bond, Vicar of Debenham; examined before the Committee sitting at Ipswich on the 10th June 1644.

I. The said Mr Bond was a constant observer of Bishop Wren's late Innovations, as bowing at the name of Jesus, reading parte of the service at the East end of the Chancell, kneeling at burialls & christnings, and inforcing such as were to be marryed to have a sacrament then, and finished the said mariages at the rayle sett up at the East end of the said chancell, and Churching woemen at the said rayle and forced them to come without their hatts to the said rayle, and did read parte of the Gospell at the Crosses in his goeing his perambulation of the said towne. (Richard Moyse, gent., John Denant).

II. The said Mr Bond in the said Wren's tyme did cause the communion table to be sett upp at the East end of the Chancell. And did cause formes to be sett by the said table before the said rayles were enioyned, and he helped to sett up the said formes himselfe & forced the comunicants to come up to the said formes. (John Denant).

III. The said Mr Bond forced his parishioners to go up to the rayles to receive the sacrament there after the said rayle was inioyned to be sett upp, to the great greife of some of his said parishioners & much trouble of their conscience; insomuch that a woman of the said parish being urged by the said Mr Bond to receive as aforesaid imediately fell sicke, complayning thereof & of the said Mr Bond to her death. (John Ashford, Richard Whiting).

IV. The said Mr Bond did putt many of his parishioners from the sacrament a whole yeer togeither because they would not go upp to the said rayles to receyve it according to Bishopp Wren's iniunctions. (Richard Moyse, Richard Whiting).

V. He affirmed & professed that he did see nothing in the oath enioyned in the late & last Canons to be taken by the Ministers but might very well be taken.[1] (Richard Moyse, John Denant, John Ward).

VI. The said Mr Bond further affirmed that Bishopp Wrenn never comanded any thinge to be donn or observed but that might be lawfully donn. And his obeying those articles & comands never troubled his conscience. (Richard Moyse).

VII. Mr Bond said, at the taking downe the comunion table from the East end of the Chancell (he being much offended thereatt), that wee should be so scrupulous now of superstition that wee should fall to playne prophannes. (Richard Shepherd).

VIII. The said Mr Bond hath expressed much bitternes & malice against the most active & best affected to the Parliament, and to their great greife since the beginning of this Parliament he wholly estrangeth himself from them,

---

[1] The reference is to the infamous 'etcetera oath', one of the provisions of the 17 canons issued by Convocation in May 1640; a manifesto of the Laudian Church, containing provocative statements on such subjects as ritual, passive obedience, and the Divine Right of Kings. For the oath and the odium aroused by it, see S. R. Gardiner, *History of England 1603–1640*, 1884, Vol. IX, pp. 143–7, 248–9.

not only discountenancinge them but reproching them with ill language, calling them Rogues & telling them they shalbe hanged if the kinge come. (Richard Moyse, John Denant, Richard Whiting).

IX. The said Mr Bond is observed to keepe company with the prophanest, & Ministers of the worst report. (Richard Moyse, Richard Shepherd).

X. The said Mr Bond since this Parliament did most maliciously on purpose read the letany & other service for this very end to offend weake consciencs, as may appeare att that tyme when one Mr Waterhouse, a godly Devine (lately come from new England),[1] being to preach in his parish on a lecture day. And James Philips further testifies that he being demanded why he did read the same then, he knowing it would much offend him, he answered he did it for the nonce or words to that effect. (Richard Moyse, Richard Shepherd).

XI. He said that the kinge was forced from the Parliament & driven to make use of the papists for his owne safety. (Richard Moyse, Richard Shepherd).

XII. He said that the Parliament must do what they list or elce they will do nothing, but the blood that is shed will lye heavy. (Richard Moyse, Richard Whiting, John Denant).

XIII. George Browne, Constable then of the said towne, demaunding payment of a rate charged upon the said Mr Bond according to an ordinance of parliament, the said Mr Bond cavilled at the payment thereof and produced to the said Constable the oath of allegiance & the oath of supremacy, and in much bitternes said that it may thanke Mr Candler & Mr Bacon of Shrubland[2] & such as they are, that so much bloud is now shed. (George Browne, jnr.).

XIV. The said Mr Bond expressed much bitternes & malignancy against the Parliament, vilifieinge and reprochinge their proceedings, sayeing that he did not know wherefore they do fight but to shed blood & kill one another. (Richard Moyse, Richard Whiting).

XV. He, the said Mr Bond, in his deske in service tyme did publish the booke for tolleration of sports in the tyme of service on a saturday. (John and Walter Denant).

XVI. (*Left blank*).

XVII. He refused to read the Parliament's declarations & warrants made upon their severall ordinancs. (Richard Whiting, George Browne, jnr.).

[1] Thomas Waterhouse. For biographical details, see Matthews, *Calamy Revised*, op. cit., p. 512. He had been assistant to Mathias Candler at Coddenham (see below, note 2) before emigrating to New England, where, in 1639, he was schoolmaster at Dorchester. After his return to England in 1643, he became schoolmaster at Colchester.

[2] Nicholas Bacon of Shrubland Hall, the elder brother of Nathaniel and Francis, the committeemen, and the Rev. Mathias Candler of the neighbouring parish of Coddenham. Besides being a notable Puritan Candler was also a student of heraldry and geneaology; in one of his collections (now Add. 15520) he described Nicholas Bacon as 'the greatest friend to pious ministers in all these parts of the country' and Shrubland Hall as 'famous for religion and hospitality'.

XVIII. That he comending of the Scotts because att their undertakings they begunn with fasting & prayer, the said Mr Bond said the Scotts were a company of cuninge Roagues. (Richard Whiting).

XIX. The said Mr Bond hath been observed seldom or never to pray for the parliament Armyes or for the Assembly of Devines; and so testifye most of his parishioners. (John Tovell, Richard Shepherd).

XX. The said Mr Bond being in talke with some of his said parishioners they asked him why he did not pray for the parliament Armyes & speake for the encouraginge of soldiers to go on in that service, he answered there was to many gonn already. (John Denant, Richard Whiting).

XXI. At the tyme of our association the said Thomas Bond was so farr from assistinge the inhabitants imployed in that service that he purposely did read in his deske a large discourse from the Cavaleers delivered to him by one Mr Henry Jenny, a graund malignant, to the great hindrance of the worke and greife to the well affected. (John Phillips, snr., Richard Shepherd, John Tovell).

XXII. The said Mr Bond did not give notice for keeping of the publiq fast accordinge to the ordinance of Parliament. (Richard Shepherd, John Tovell, Henry Blomfield).

XXIII. The said Mr Bond hath often affirmed that if he were as Mr Withers of Wetheringsett or Mr Hill of Thornedon (which were two ministers outed for their scandalous lives & doctrine)[1] that he would not care a pynn for they should soon be sett in agen, he would warrant them, with credit, or words to that purpose. (Richard Shepherd).

XXIV. The said Mr Bond did not take the late vow & covenant first set forth by this present Parliament, but did much hinder those that would by his doctrine, sayeing in his sermon that he was not satisfied that the King did fight to maynteyn popery and they that were might take it if they please, and so refused to take it. (Richard Moyse, Richard Shepherd, John Tovell).

XXV. The said Mr Bond being solicited at severall tymes by the well affected in his parish to come in and give publicke satisfaction to the Inhabitants of the said towne of his correspondency to the Parliament's proceedinges, or otherwise they must exhibite Articles against him, he badd them go on & do their worst for he cared not what could be donn unto him. (Richard Shepherd, John Tovell, John Denant, Richard Whiting, Henry Blomfield).

The living is worth £70 per annum, and he has £20 per annum temporal estate; Bond has no children.

1644 10th June: Proved before Nathaniel Bacon, William Bloys, Peter Fisher, Robert Duncon, John Base.

Manchester's warrant for the ejection of Bond is undated and undirected.

[1] William Withers, Rector of Wetheringsett and John Hill, Rector of Thorndon. No record of the charges against either of these ministers has survived.

More articles besids the former which we still maynteyne against Robert Large (*Large was curate of Charsfield, the village from which these witnesses came, and curate of Hoo and Letheringham*).

I. That the said Mr Large, notwithstanding the admonition from this Committee, he continues his former way of readinge upon the Lord's dayes & fast dayes parte of a booke used in the Bishops' tymes & imposed by them to be read on fast dayes in the time of the great sicknes. (Lionel Roydon, Thomas Borne, Lionel Bradstreet).

II. That the said Mr Large is an alehousehanter. (Thomas Borne, Lionel Cornish).

III. That the said Mr Large hath been drunke at the blew boare in Wickham markett and divers tymes at Letheringham Abbey, and once at Dallinghoo he was so drunke that he fell into the fire, & that he hath been distempered divers tymes beside with beere or wyne. Thomas Brookes saw him fall into the fire. Anthony Burwood saw him fall into the fire & afterwards into a bush, having drunke, as he supposed, to much. (Anthony Burwood, Lionel Bradstreet, Thomas Borne, Lionel Cornish).

1644 5th August: proved before Francis Bacon, William Bloys, John Base, Peter Fisher, Robert Duncon.

That the said Mr Large did take the vow & covenant with theis words, Ego Robertus Large, Curate, ibidem quatenus de iure subscribo, Robert Large. As per the annexed certificat.[1]

Manchester's warrant for the ejection of Large is undated and undirected.

Articles against Henry Rolinson, Vicar of Bawdsey and Rector of Hollesley.

I. That he was a constant observer of the late superstitious Innovations; amonge the rest goeing upp to the rayles and elevating the bread & wyne at the words of consecration at the tyme of administring of the sacrament; hath refused to give thanks after the childbirth of woemen (vizt. of one Foxe's wife & others) because they would not come upp to the rayles as was inoyned. And he hath refused to baptize children if they came not with such a number of godfathers & godmothers as was enioyned by the Bishopps; and att a tyme, because one of the godfathers would not stand by, he was so vexed & troubled in mynde that he would not preach, alleadging that to be the cause of his not preaching at that tyme. (Charles Smith, George Warren, Edward Archer, William Warren, Robert Chandler, Nathaniel Salins, Jeremy Coleman, Francis Mersey).

II. That he sleighted & neglected the monethly fast and also upon a conference with some of his neighbours upon a fast day he said Why are not the diggers at worke ? & one replyeing It was fast day, he scornefully then said Tush, that was nothing, it was made by man and they might worke on that

[1] Large subscribed the Covenant only as far as the law allowed.

day, & [he] sett his owne men to worke on that day. (John Bolton, Francis Batram, William Stock [or Starke], William Warren).

III. That he refused to take the first vow & covenant, sayeing it did not concerne him. (George Warren, Edward Archer).

IV. That being demanded why he prayed in his prayer before sermon for ArchBishopps, [and] Bishopps, they being voted out of this Parliament, he said that Parliament's votes were no law. (John Cockson, John Harrison, Edward Archer).

V. That he did read the booke of liberty for sports on the lord's day, and setts to officiate the Cure att Baudsey one Smith, a scandalous & ill affected Parson, & such like. (Edward Archer, Nathaniel Salins, Jeremy Coleman).

VI. That the surplice being taken & laid in the pulpitt, he very angerly demanded where it was, & thretned to have them that stole it hold upp their hands at the barr, & so then he did read service without it. (Edward Archer, Jeremy Coleman).

VII. That he hath been distempered with excesse of beere & wyne. (John Ford, Edward Archer, Jeremy Coleman).

VIII. That he said that those that beare sway in the Parliament were Brownists & Anabaptists. (Nathaniel Salins).

IX. That when he was tendring the nationall covenant he said that by schisme was meant devision & those Conventicle lecturers that seeke houses & corners to preach in, and those we are to oppose & stand against; & speaking of the word prophannes he quoted Ecclesiastes, cap. 8 & verse 4, after which words he said What nobleman, what Peere can say to the king what doest thou? and you see, said he, it is not my words but the word of God, therefore you must not in the least way oppose or withstand the king's command. And he used many like expressions to engage the people against the Parliament. (George Warren, William Stock, Charles Smith).

1644 2nd April: Proved before William Bloys, Peter Fisher, Robert Brewster, Francis Brewster, Robert Duncon, John Base.

A Reply to the Answer of Henry Rolinson.

I. That the said Mr Rolleison did approve of the late Inovations may appeare by his practise, vizt. that he did elevate the bread & wyne as in the said article. (Charles Smith, Robert Chandler).

That he refused to give thanks after the childbirth of women as in the said Article, the rayles then standing, & amonge the rest Foxe's wife, upon such refusall, went away not givinge thanks. (Thomas Buttolph, John Bolton, Francis Batram).

Joyner testifieth that the rayles were sett upp by Mr Rolleison his directions & approbations, and that his servants and he being about to breake the ground to place the railes, the said Mr Rolleison did forbidd them so to do.

There was no rayles sett upp at Baudsey because no place there convenient, yett there was a chancell doore made and the table sett alterwise by Mr Rolleison his directions. (Edward Archer, Robert Chandler).

II. To the 2nd., that he sleighted & neglected the monethly fast. (John Bolton). Thomas Buttolph also testifieth that he hath seen Mr Rolleison his servants att cart on the fast day. Concerning the conference, affirmatively as in the said article.

III. To the 3rd., affirmatively as in the article. (Edward Archer, Thomas Buttolph).

IV. To the 4th, affirmatively as in the article; & further it is conceyved by him to be confessed in substance though not in words. (Edward Archer, John Cockson, John Harrison).

V. To the 5th. That Mr Rolleison his Curat Mr Smith is a man of ill fame & report and further the said Mr Smith is an alehouse haunter & frequenter of tavernes, and hath been often distempered with excesse of beere or wyne. (Edward Archer).

VI. To the 6th, affirmatively as in the Article. (Edward Archer, Jeremy Coleman).

VII. To the 7th testifies that he hath been often distempered with excesse of beere or wyne. (Edward Archer).

VIII. To the 8th affirmatively as in the Article. John Fox saith that Mr Rolleison said that wee were forward to give their money awaye to maynteyne Brownists & Anabaptists. (Nathaniel Salins).

IX. To the 9th. affirmatively as in the article. And further proved by Thomas Buttolph, William Harman, & William Harward. (Charles Smith).

This replication was brought in the (   ) [sic] August 1644: Francis Bacon, William Bloys, John Base, Peter Fisher, Robert Duncon.

Manchester's warrant for the ejection of Rolinson is undated and undirected. In the summer of 1647 Rolinson was summoned before the Westminster Committee of Plundered Ministers for harassing John Wilkinson who had replaced him at Hollesley. It is clear that on this occasion he received a good deal of support from his parish.[1]

Articles against William Proctor, Rector of Stradishall.

I. That the said Mr Procter hath beine a strict & zealous observer & mainteyner of the late Innovations & Ceremonyes in the Church. Videlicit: preachinge in his surplise & hood, useinge noe other prayer before his sermons then the biddinge Cannonicall prayer, and kneeleinge at buryalls & marrieinge, & Churchinge of women at the Rayles, standinge up at Glorie be to the father; hee read the second service at the Alter both before & after his sermons. (William Owats [or Owers], Joshua Paske [M][2], Thomas Pament [M]).

II. That the said Mr Procter, about five or six yeares since upon a Communion day, requireinge the said deponants to come up to the rayles to receive

[1] Add. 15671, ff. 156v, 210, 229, 237.
[2] All the witnesses sign their names except those distinguished by an 'M', who are marksmen.

the sacrament (they beinge then in the Chancell in theire seats ready to receive), one of them answered Our consciences will not suffer us to come up, whereupon hee said hee would satisfie our consciences & said further that our names should be returned to the Court and wee should pay dearly for it. (Joshua Paske, Susan Paske [M]).

III. This deponent Joshua Paske afterwards went to Mr Procter & desired him to write a letter to the Court that his neighbours that were put into the Court might be befreinded, whereupon hee, the said Mr Procter, did write a letter to Dr Eden[1] by reason whereof (as the said deponents beleive) two of his parishoners, videlicet, Susan Paske was suspended six weeks or thereabouts, & one Edmund Stoakham was soe prosecuted with excommunication that hee was faine to fly out of the Country. Then presently after the Iudge sayeinge to these deponents Have you beine exhorted by your minister in publique & private & will you not be ruled? and then hee askeinge whoe was our minister, Mr Coleman the Regester answered That is Mr Procter, as conformable a man as any is in our diosesse. (Joshua & Susan Paske).

IV. That the said Mr Procter did exhort these deponants in private to come up to the Rayle to receive the sacrament, alledginge unto them the Comaund of God in the 13 Romans I:2 Let every soule be subject to the higher powers etc. And then said further if yee resist you shall receive damnation. (Joshua and Susan Paske, Elizabeth French [M].

V. That the said Mr Procter after the Rayles were taken away did (as theise deponents beleive) cause the formes to be sett round about the Communion table, & there hee went in & called his parishoners to come up thither & there hee did administer the sacrament to his parishoners. (Thomas Pament, John Dere, Henry French & divers others).

VI. That the said Mr Procter in the time of Innovations & Ceremonyes did preach in his sermons that his parishoners were bound to give thanks to god that they had the word severely taught unto them and the ordinances in the Purity of them. (Thomas Pament, Joshua and Susan Paske).

VII. That the said Mr Procter did deliver in a sermon upon a sunday in the forenoone about 2 yeares since that Jobe did curse God, & in the afternoone of the same day hee said again that for want of faith Job did curse & blaspheme God to his very face. (Thomas Pament, Joshua and Susan Paske).

VIII. That the said Mr Procter in a sermon about 2 yeares since did lay all the Curses mentioned in the Epistle of Jude from the 11th to the 19th verse thereof unto the Chardge of those that went abroad to heare pious Ministers sayeinge that sermon goers were the worst of all sorts of People & further said that it was they & none but they that brought these troubles upon the times. (William Owats, Thomas Pament, Susan Paske).

[1] Thomas Eden, Ll.D., a famous civil lawyer, Master of Trinity Hall, Chancellor of the Diocese of Ely and Commissary for Bury St. Edmunds and Sudbury in the 1630s. In 1640 he was elected as M.P. for Cambridge University. Despite his previous activities in the Ecclesiastical Courts, he remained at Westminster until his death in 1645, making several donations to the Parliamentary cause and taking the Solemn League and Covenant. (See D.N.B.)

IX. That the said Mr Procter in the same sermon did utter these words or the like in effect, videlicet: I will shake the dust of my feete against you & as it was said of Babilon soe I will doe unto you for I will reward you double; & further said You have sinned five manner of wayes, against God, against Authority, against the Church, against mee, & against your owne soules; sayeinge sermon goers were the worst of all kind of people & that hee had heard Forty say soe. (Joshua and Susan Paske).

X. That the said Mr Procter did read the booke of sports for the prophana- tion of the saboth openly in the Church as hee hath confessed himselfe to this depondent Thomas French. (William Owats, Thomas French).

XI. This deponent hath seene the said Mr Procter hedginge upon a saboth day. (Thomas Pament; his wife can testifie this, but shee is sicke).

XII. That the said Mr Procter about halfe a yeare since did suffer his ser- vants to hedge upon a fast day, contrary to the Ordinance of Parliament. (Thomas Bowyer).

XIII. This deponant hath seene his maide servant bake upon a fast day. (Susan Paske).

XIV. That the said Mr Procter is a common swearer, & hath sworne by his faith & troth in the heareinge of this deponent Thomas Pament & hath sworne As God Judge mee in the heareinge of this deponent Daniel French. (Daniel French, Thomas Pament).

XV. That the said Mr Procter hath suffered much Card playeinge in his house night after night, & hath seene 4 paire of Cards goeinge at one time in his house. (William Perman).

XVI. The said Mr Procter hath a paire of nine holes in his house & hath set some of his parish to play at them. (Thomas Bowyer).

XVII. That the said Mr Procter six yeares since or thereabouts did take one Mr Mortlock to his house & there hee was made drunke & then hee came into the feild with the said Mr Mortlock, & Mr Mortlock beinge soe drunke that hee tumbled up & downe upon the ground [and] the said Mr Procter stood & laught at him. (John Dere).

XVIII. That the said Mr Procter is an Alehouse haunter & came out of an Alehouse Rayleinge of a man & calleinge him Rascall & knave & (   ) [sic]. And hath seene him with disordered and drunken company. (William and Margaret Perman).

XIX. That these deponents did see the said Mr Procter (as hee was comeinge from Hundon-ward) soe disguised in drinke that hee could scarce sitt on his horseback, but was ready to fall downe of his horse. (John and Anne Dere).

XX. That these deponents have heard the said Mr Procter tell divers bawdy tales soe prophane & uncivill as was neither fitt for modest tounge or eare to speake or heare (unfittinge for a Minister or any other) at such time as he had beine drinkinge two or three howers togeather at the least. And hee hath heard bawdy tales told & would not reprove the party that told them. (William Chapman, Susan Paske).

XXI. That Mr Procter hath suffered diverse scandalous Ministers to preach in his Church, videlicet one Mr Choate, who (as these deponents have heard) was convicted at the Sessions for beinge a common drunkard, & one Mr Humfrey, who went away with another man's wife. (Joshua and Susan Paske).

XXII. That Mr Procter hath denyed to lett one Mr Blakaby, a godly minister preach in his Church although hee was earnestly intreated to doe it by William Barker, & said hee had a comaund to the contrary. (William Barker).

XXIII. That this deponent's wife beinge brought to bedd, & the child beinge very weake this deponent went to Mr Procter & desired him to Christen his child for him. The said Mr Procter answered that hee would not Christen it untill hee listed, soe that this deponent was forced to goe to another towne to gett a minister to Christen his Child. Alsoe at another time upon a friday this deponent's wife haveinge 2 children at a birth, they beinge very weake this deponent went to the said Mr Procter & desired & earnestly intreated him to Christen them & told him that they were soe weake they were like to dye. Hee then told this deponent hee would not Christen them untill Saboth day followeinge in the afternoone, & although this deponent went againe & his wife sent a neighbour to intreate the said Mr Procter to baptize the said 2 children, hee would not doe it, by reason whereof one of the children dyed unbaptized & the other beinge carried out to the Church upon the sunday to be baptized it beinge weake & the weather cold & Mr Procter would not come to the house to baptize it soe it dyed that Sonday at night after it was baptized, which this deponent beleives was a greate cause of the child's death. (Thomas French).

XXIV. This deponent haveinge a child to be Christned and liveinge a mile of from the Church it was carried to the Church to be baptized upon a Sonday in the afternoone, & because it came not soon enough (as Mr Procter pretended) hee would not baptize it but sent it away unbaptized although the truth is the child was brought into the Church before hee went into the pulpitt. (Thomas Sharpe).

XXV. That Mr Procter did deny to baptize one Beniamin Smythe's child because it came not before the second lesson was read although hee was earnestly intreated by his parishoners to doe it, & turned it away unbaptized. (Jane Bowyer, Thomas Sharpe).

XXVI. That the said Mr Procter did marry one Anne Geu to one Henry Hurst in her owne house; within 4 dayes after shee was delivered of a base child (as he hath confessed himselfe to this deponent, Thomas French), and hee Churched her & received her to the Sacrament without any publique confession that the said deponants knowe or have heard of. (Thomas French, Thomas Sharpe).

XXVII. That Mr Procter hath kept one Susan Serjeant whoe had comitted the like sinne of whoredome from the punishment of the Law (although it was reported shee had her child by her owne father) by speakeinge for her to Sir William Soames & other Justices of the peace, although there was a warrant out against her. (William Chapman, Joshua Paske, Thomas French).

XXVIII. That Mr Procter sent for this deponent & said these words or the like in effect to this deponent, You told mee that Thomas Bowyer & his mother fell out & hee beate her & misused her & shee sickned & dyed upon it. This deponent answered hee did never say any such thinge, whereupon Mr Procter replyed in a furious manner, You did. Then presently after this deponent said to him, I marvile you will urge any man to forsweare himselfe. Then Mr Procter said If you will say those words I will beare your chardgs. Then this deponent answered againe, I wonder that [a] man of your cloth would induce a man to forswere himselfe. (John Coe).

XXIX. That the said Mr Procter is a man much given to opression; hee did take 5/- for a trespas done by 2 bullocks in a fallow land. (William Chapman, Thomas Bowyer).

XXX. That this deponent did owe the said Mr Procter 2/4d and, although hee promised to pay it him within 3 or 4 dayes or a weeke, hee putt him into the Court & made it cost this deponent 22/- for chardges beside his jorney to Bury although hee paid his debt upon the Court day morninge. Although hee then did & still doth owe unto this deponent John Deere 2/6d for five loads of muck. (John and Anne Dere).

XXXI. This deponent beinge a poore man & haveing noe worke at home was forced to seeke out for worke & went to Newmarkett where hee wrought two yeares at least; & because this deponent came not home to Church every Sonday Mr Procter caused this deponent to be excommunicated, & the Court seeinge the cause unjust, & that it was done out of spleene, they wished this deponent to meete them at Hawdon[1] Church & there they would absolve him, which was done accordingly. (John Coe).

XXXII. These deponents have heard Abraham Serjeant confesse that Mr Procter did sett him to steale yonge plants out of other men's grounds, both Ashes & Crabstocks. (Thomas Prigge, Thomas Bowyer, John Dere).
Serjeant is a lame man but will come if neede be to swere to this himselfe.

XXXIII. These deponents have heard one Goody Owers, whoe is now sick, [say] that she told Mr Procter of his tipleinge & drinkinge & keepinge company. Then the said Mr Procter said it was the fashion of [the] tymes to set the Barrill of Ale one end. Then shee answered, Woe be to him that gives his neighbour drinke to make him drunke; hee then answered, I (as the apostle saith) doe become all thinges to all that I may win some. (William Owers, Susan Paske).

XXXIV. That the said Mr Procter about Christmas last did give a trooper soe much Beere at his house that hee made him almost drunke; hee drew the beere himselfe. The trooper confessed that hee was a jovyall smooth tonged parson, or words to the like effect, & hee had 20 such at Lynn in prison. (Thomas and Anne Bowyer, Joshua and Susan Paske).

---

[1] Presumably Hawkedon.

XXXV. There is soe many other thinges against the said Mr Procter that if wee should enter into particuler wronges wee should be a longe time in relateinge them. (Joshua Paske, William Chapman, John Dere, John Coe, William Perman).

The living, whose patron is the Earl of Devonshire, is valued at about £100 per annum; Procter has £20 per annum temporal means, but pays £12 per annum from this during the life of an old bed-ridden woman. He has a wife and three children.

1644 12th April: before the Comissioners for scandalous Ministers sittinge at Cambridge for the seaven associated Countyes:- Dudley Pope, Robert Castell, Robert Clarke, Thomas French, Robert Robson.

Manchester's warrant for the ejection of Proctor is undated and undirected.

Articles against Philip Parsons, Vicar of Great Finborough.

I. That Mr Parsons hath beine absent from his Cure these twleve monthes & upwards, & hath beine & is still in actuall warr against the Parliament as they have beine informed. (Edmund Skipp, Robert Rant, Robert Abbott, Edward Syer).

II. That Mr Parsons did wilfully & constantly refuse to pay the payment of taxes inposed upon him by the Parliament & said it was against his Conscience. (John Sherwood).

III. That Mr Parsons did constantly bow to the rayles & was a strict observer & promoter of Bishopp Wren's Innovations. (Robert Crosse, Edmund Skipp, Robert Abbott, Edward Syer).

IV. That when the stepps were sett up before the Alter (which were three) Mr Parsons named the first stepp the father, the second the sonne, & the third stepp the holy ghost, & bowed to them all severally. (Elias Scofield, Robert Rant).

1644 [*i.e. 1645*] 21st January: Proved before: Francis Bacon, Sir William Spring, Brampton Gurdon, snr., Brampton Gurdon, jnr., Thomas Chaplin.

Manchester's warrant for the ejection of Parsons, which is undirected, is dated the 5th February 1645.

Depositions against John Brown, Rector of Moulton.

(*Witness:* George Moody).

To the first hee saith that in his opinion the said John Browne is a very weake preacher & very insufficient to performe his function.

To the second hee saith the said Mr Browne never preached in theire parish upon any fast day untill now of late neither hath hee heard him preach at any time upon the fift of November.

To the third hee saith that the said John Browne for want of instructinge of his parishoners of the nature of a fast & of the Lord's day they are Ignorant of theire dutyes towards God & follow their worke, labor, & other imployments, as bakeinge upon the fast & Lord's day. And the said Mr Browne passeinge by the youth upon the Lord's day they beinge at play would not rebuke them for it.

To the fourth hee saith that the said John Browne for the space of these 30 yeares now last path hath preached but once a day upon the Lord's day. And that at some times, when hee doth not preach, in stead of a sermon hee reads the Bishopps' Cannons.

To the fift hee saith that the said John Browne did read the booke of sports set forth for the prophanation of the saboth in the Church to the parishoners, although some of his parishoners did desire him to forbeare & they would save him harmles for the same.

To the sixt hee saith that the said John Browne was a strict observer of Bishopp Wren his Injunctions & Innovations, as boweinge at the name of Jesus, & urgeinge the people to come up to the Rayles, and doth still marry, bury and Church women in a superstitious way as readinge & walkinge from the Church gate to the grave before the dead corps and goeinge to the stoole end in the Church where women sitt to Church them.

To the nineth hee saith that the said John Browne doth not publiquely pray for a blessinge upon the parliament's proceedings nor the assembly of divines, navy at Sea nor forces by land.

To the Tenth hee saith that the said Mr Browne is a Gamster & useth to play at Cardes & Tables & doth associate himself with swearers, Alehousehaunters, & others ill affected parsons to the parliament, and disrespecteth the well affected in his parish.

To the eleventh, that upon the day of thanksgiveinge for discovery of a dangerous designe intended against the Parliament & Citty of London the said Mr John Browne preached, but hee said hee knew not for what, for they talked of a deliverance but hee knew of none.

To the XIIth hee deposeth & saith that the said Mr Browne hath slightly read the Ordinances sent downe by the Parliament to be read in the Church, & instead of stirringe up the people to contribute freely hee hath discouridged them & given them badd example, as after hee had read the Ordinance for the Lord Fairefax to his parishoners hee had done with it and soe there was nothinge gathered.

To the thirteenth hee saith that the said Mr Browne did refuse to ioyne in findinge Associated Armes, and beinge required to subscribe what hee would doe in it, hee answered Shall I find armes against my Kinge.

To the sixteenth hee deposeth & saith that about a yeare since hee heard the said Mr Browne say that hee wished the times were as good now as formerly when wee paid ship money.

(signed) George Moodye.

(Thomas White).

To the second: (*as Moody*).

To the third:(*as Moody – but omitting Brown's refusal to rebuke the young people of the town as he walked by them while they were at play on the Sabbath*).

To the fifth: (*as Moody – but omitting the request made to him by some of his parishioners that he should desist from reading the Book of Sports*).

To the sixth: (*as Moody*).

To the tenth: (*swears to the truth of the Article*).

To the eleventh: (*swears to the truth of the Article*).

To the Twelfth: (*swears to the truth of the Article*).

The mark of Thomas White.

(Richard Prick).

To the sixth: (*swears that the Article is true in every particular*).

To the eight hee saith that the said Mr Browne doth not examine his parishoners before the receiveinge of the sacrament of the Lord's supper, whether they be fittinge to come to the Ordinance or not, but admitteth of any, though Ignorant or prophane.

To the ninth: (*as Moody*).

To the tenth: (*as is set down in the Article*).

To the twelth: (*as is set down in the Article*).

To the sixteenth hee deposeth & saith that hee heard Mr Browne wish that the tymes were now as formerly when wee paid shipmoney & said likewise, I would wee had peace one way or other.

(signed) Richard Prick.

(Robert Nonne).

To the fourteenth: hee saith that above a yeare since the Question beinge put to Mr Browne whether side were right, meaneinge the Kinge or Parliament, hee answered the Parliament was naught. And hee further saith that same day Mr Browne was distempered with drinke & went home late at night.

(signed) Robert Nonne.

(Edmund Carver).

To the XIIIIth. hee saith that hee might aske the question to Mr Browne whether either side were right, meaneinge the Kinge or Parliament, but cannot call to mind the answere of the said Mr Browne. And hee further saith that the said Mr Browne was drinkinge with him at Newmarkett at the same time and went home late at night.

(signed) Edmond Carver.

(Jonas Alston).

To the first: (*as Moody*).

To the eighth: (*swears to the truth of the article*).

To the ninth: (*as Moody*).

(signed) Jonas Alston.

(Richard Rayner).

To the second: (*as Moody*).

To the fourth: (*as Moody*).

To the fifteenth hee saith that the said Mr Browne upon the Lord's day passeinge by and behouldinge the youth of the towne at play in this deponent's presence hee did not rebuke them for the same.

The mark of Richard Rayner.

(William Clerke).

To the fourth: (*as Moody*).

To the ninth: (*as Moody*).

The mark of William Clerke.

The living is worth £40 per annum; Browne is a bachelor, and his personal estate is valued at £100.

1644 14th November: proved before Thomas Tirrell, Robert Brewster, Francis Brewster, Samuel Moody, Thomas Chaplin.

Manchester's warrant for the ejection of Brown, which is undirected, was issued on the 17th March 1645.

II

The Case of William Keeble, Rector of Ringshall

Keeble, Rector of the parish of Ringshall since 1613, was first attacked in November 1643, when two of his parishioners, Thomas Cooper and Thomas Gibbon, presented eight articles against him to the Committee of Plundered Ministers at Westminster. The Committee heard the evidence and were about to pass judgement, presumably in favour of Keeble, when his prosecutors claimed that they could produce new material and petitioned that the case be referred to Manchester. The Westminster Committee agreed to this, and on the 2nd April 1644 Keeble's opponents exhibited 13 Articles against him to the Ipswich Committee for Scandalous Ministers (Document 1). On the 15th of that month Keeble returned his Answer to these Articles and was ready with witnesses to prove his case, but the Committee claimed that they had no authority to receive these proofs. Thereupon Keeble petitioned Manchester, enclosing a copy of his Answer. As a result of this appeal the Earl ordered that the prosecutors should be given a copy of the Rector's Answer, to which they might reply, and, if they so desired, present more Articles against Keeble. On the 22nd July Keeble's opponents appeared before the Ipswich Committee, and not only made a Replication to his Answer, but added some new charges against the Rector (Document 2). Without waiting for Keeble to make any reply to the new material, the Committee forwarded the case to Manchester, and got a sequestration issued against the Rector; Keeble later claimed that this was obtained by some underhand dealing by Peter Fisher, who "had offered the living to a brother in law of his."[1] Certainly when Keeble petitioned the Earl complaining of the injustice of the Committee's actions, Manchester revoked his order of sequestration and instructed the Committee to hear the Rector's Answers to the Articles, examine his witnesses, and then make a full report of the case (Document 3). The Committee performed the first two parts of Manchester's order, but then failed to return their report to the Earl; as a result Keeble petitioned the Earl again (Document 4), desiring that the Committee should return their report swiftly and that he would appoint a day when both sides might be heard before him in London. Manchester agreed to Keeble's suggestion, but, lacking the opportunity to hear the case himself, referred it to White, the Chairman of the Westminster Committee of Plundered Ministers, and to Samuel Smith, the Steward of the City of Norwich, for their final determination. White and Smith reviewed the case, and the latter[2] certified their joint opinion that

---

[1] Ms. J. Walker, c. 7, f. 167.

[2] A further complication added to Keeble's misfortunes as White died after he and Smith had examined the case, but before they could make their joint report.

there was no cause for sequestration to the Earl, who confirmed Keeble in his living on the 24th January 1645 (Document 5). But the Rector's opponents were not easily discouraged; in March they presented 7 further Articles, consisting largely of a reworking of the previous charges, to Manchester, but the latter only ratified his January order, telling one of the prosecutors "that hee did not think it iust that Mr Keble should be any further molested but be fynally dismissed as to any old matter." Even this was not the end of Keeble's persecution. In July 1645, after the termination of Manchester's authority in such cases, the Rector's opponents exhibited 19 Articles against him to the Westminster Committee for Plundered Ministers,[1] which the latter referred to the Ipswich Committee, for examination. Keeble petitioned that these Articles were substantially the same as those previously presented to Manchester, of which he had been found innocent; the Westminster Committee examined this claim, and, finding that the Articles were "the same in substance with the former articles", dismissed Keeble from any further prosecution.

Some reasons for the success of Keeble's defence against such determined opposition may be suggested. Most materially, none of the acid-tests of 'malignancy' were positive in Keeble's case; as he claimed in his petition to Manchester, he had "taken the protestation, the association, the nationall League & Covenant, & hath paid his fift & 20th part & all other Parliament Cessis & taxis." Judgement had to be made on more subjective criteria, and clearly a substantial party existed in Keeble's parish who supported their Rector and were prepared to give evidence in his behalf to negate the effect of the prosecution's testimonies. But equally important was the competent handling of the case by Keeble's 'solicitor', his brother Richard. The latter was a lawyer of some reputation before the Civil War, who was to rise to a position of eminence under the Commonwealth as one of the Commissioners of the Great Seal.[2] It seems probable that Richard had well-placed friends at Westminster, and this would explain the exceptional access he had to Manchester and to the central Committee when pressing his brother's case.[3]

Document 1 (*from the Lincoln City Library Ms.*)

Articles against William Keeble, Rector of Ringshall, presented the 2nd April 1644 to the Committee at Ipswich (Nathaniel Bacon, Francis Bacon, Francis Brewster, Robert Brewster, Peter Fisher, Robert Duncon).

I. That the said Mr Keeble did strictly observe & practice Bishopp Wren's Iniunctions; among the rest goeing upp to the rayles, churchinge women there, urging them with threats to come upp thither, affirming that they were sett upp by lawfull authority. And refused to give the sacrament of the

---

[1] Ms. J. Walker, c. 7, f. 164v.

[2] Richard Keeble is the subject of an article in the Dictionary of National Biography. See also J. J. Muskett, *Suffolk Manorial Families*, Vol. 2 (Exeter, 1908), pp. 271–9.

[3] This account is based on those documents printed in the following section, and on Ms. J. Walker, c. 7, ff. 166, 170.

Lord's supper to those that would not come upp to the rayle to receyve the same, though Richard Manninge & Thomas Cooper satt in a seat so neer that he might have reached it to them. (Richard Manning, Thomas Cooper, Bridget Cooper).

II. That the said Mr Keeble, Anno 1641, in his sermon extolled Bishopp Wren's Innovations, and said that it was better to observe bad orders then no orders. Now (said he) every man will deny the pope and yett be a pope himselfe to say & doe what he list. (Richard Manning, John Bixby).

III. That the said Mr Keeble, contrary to the ordinance of Parliament, hath exceedingly neglected the monethly fast, affirminge it to be a tyme of feastinge not of fastinge; bitterly inveighing against such as resort to other parish Churches to keepe the fast, sayeing they had rather go heare such as rayled in the pulpett 4 or 5 houres then heare him (albeit he himselfe kept not the fast). (Thomas Cooper, John Bixby, Thomas Gibbon, Ambrose Bixby).

IV. The said Mr Keeble for the most parte in the pulpett readeth verbatim all that he delivereth, and haveing a sett number of sermons keepeth his constant rounds yeere after yeere. (Thomas Cooper, Joseph Crossett).

V. That the said Mr Keeble bitterly inveighing in his sermons against godly & paynfull ministers said that if a minister can but gett upp into a pulpitt or tubb & speake earnestly for the parliament, those are the onely men now adayes though they be Coblers or tinkers. (Thomas Cooper, Ralph Hall).

VI. That the said Mr Keeble being required to contribute for the mayntenance of the warres raised for the defence of the Parliament, he said that it did not stand with the feare of god to give maintenance or to lift up his hand against the prince. But now, said he, the land is grown to such a passe that such a company are gathered togeither that will either have a kinge of one of themselves or elce of their owne setting upp though the land swym with blood. And further to shew his ill will to the Parliament, he said that a papist offered to rayse forcs for the kinge [*and*] the kinge refused him because he was a papist, but the Parliament did offer a great some of money to obteyne his service, which the kinge hearinge off did then enterteyne him. And to cast an everlastinge blott upon the parliament he said they putt the Earle of Strafford to death wrongefully. (Thomas & Bridget Cooper, Ambrose Bixby, Thomas Grymwade).

VII. That the said Mr Keeble refused to read bookes comanded to be read by ordinance of Parliament, among which that for raisinge money, horse & plate, and also the Remonstrance & others. And in his sermon, intimatinge those or the like bookes, he scornefully said if every pamphlett should be read in the church it would spend all the tyme appointed for devyne service, or to that effect. (Ambrose Bixby, Richard Manning, Thomas Gibbon, Richard Driver, Bassingbourn Cooper).

VIII. That the said Mr Keeble refused to take the first vow & covenant, and hindred others sayeing in his sermon the very bramble now would be above the Cedar, adding that he would not take the said covenant as others did for £100. (Thomas Cooper, Thomas Gibbon, Ambrose Bixby).

IX. That he refused to associate on behalfe of King & Parliament, and there uppon leavinge his parish 3 weekes fled to a noted papist's house (viz.) att Flixam hall, neer Leistoffe,[1] (as himselfe confessed). And his usuall associats ar either papists or notorious malignants or ill affected persons (viz.) Nash, Baldry, Bretton & the like. Neither would he lend or give any thinge to the Parliament but what he hath been compelled unto, wherefore his horses have been twice taken from him. (Richard Manning, Thomas Cooper, Ambrose Bixby).

X. That the said Mr Keeble about the beginning of this unnaturall warr, being told what a number the Kinge had gathered togeither against the Parliament wished that the Kinge had as many more. (Ambrose Bixby, Ralph Hall).

XI. That the said Mr Keeble when the knights of the shire for this County of Suffolk were chosen did scornefully say that none did chuse them but leathercoats, scarecrows and squirell hunters, or words to the like effect. (Francis Manning, Edward Cooke).

XII. That he hath not tendered the nationall Covenant according to the ordinance of Parliament. Omittinge parte of it and suffering some to subscribe to an imperfect roll that were not at the readinge of the said covenant; and it is credibly reported that he hath tendered it to some at private houses. This covenant was delivered to him about a moneth since, and some subscribed it in the afternoone who were not present at the readinge of it in the forenoon. (Thomas Cooper, Ralph Hall, James Harlond).

XIII. I can testify that I beinge at the said Keeble's house when he absented himselfe for feare of beinge taken for a malignant, I searched for armes and in his study upon the table I saw divers pamphlets and they were all invective against the Parliament, but not one to be found from or on the behalfe of the Parliament. (Samuel Duncon).

The living is worth £120 per annum.

Document 2 (*from the Lincoln City Library Ms.*).

A Reioynder to Mr William Keeble his answer to certen Articles exhibited against him to the Committee of plundered Ministers. *The Rejoinder was presented to the Ipswich Committee (Nathaniel Bacon, William Bloys, Francis Bacon, Peter Fisher, Robert Duncon) on the 22nd July 1644.*

I. Whereas he saith he was no strict observer of Bishopp Wren's Iniunctions, we averr he was, and did very strictly observe them; and did refuse to church any women except they came upp to the rayles and except they came upp without a hatt and did also urge them to come upp to the rayles . . . (Elizabeth Hicks, Ruth Wellam, Bridget Cooper) . . . And did refuse to give the

---

[1] The witnesses have confused their geography in this article: Keeble did not flee to the parish of Flixton near Lowestoft, but to Flixton Hall in South Elmham, the home of the recusant Lady Tasborough.

sacrament except they came upp to the rayles and did affirme that the table was sett upp by lawfull authority . . . (Thomas & Bridget Cooper, Richard Manning) . . . And did also bowe goeing upp to the rayles . . . (James Harlewyne, Thomas Cooper).

II. Wee averr he did extoll Bishopp Wren's Innovations as is proved already upon oath. (Richard Manning, Thomas Cooper).

III. When he did keepe any fast dayes he did read or preach but one sermon a day and for the fast that fell on the 28th of December 1642 he said the saboath before that he was to give them notice of a fast on Wensday next, but it was contradicted by a superior law and therefore was to be kept as a feast & not as a fast; expressinge himselfe further that lett others do as they would, but he for his parte would not keepe it. And Thomas Cooper & Richard Maninge testify that he blamed his parishioners for hearinge other ministers, who he said (though falsely) rayled in the pulpitt foure or five houres. (Thomas Cooper, Thomas Gibbon, Ambrose Bixby, John Bixby, Thomas Wellam, Henry Betts).

IV. Wee averr that he doth for the most parte read verbatim all that he delivereth, keepinge his round yeere after yeere. (Thomas Cooper, Thomas Skudgen, Thomas Wellam, Thomas Gibbon).

V. He did inveigh against godly & paynfull Ministers using the very words that are mentioned in the 5th article. And likewise he said that those that went to heare other godly ministers were like merchants that were at great charge to sett out a shipp & bring home none but apes, munkyes &c. (Thomas Cooper, Ralph Hall, Thomas Gibbon).

VI. He did not associate untill 3 weekes after warninge was given duringe which tyme he absented himselfe till he could noe longer be hid. As for his settinge forth of a soldier, it is a small thing for a man of his estate that had £180 per annum in spirituall & temporall, when some of his neighbours that had not above £14 or £15 per annum did twice as much. As for his subscription of £10 or an horse, he did not pay till halfe a yeere after, when the Parliament troopers came to take his horse & armes for the money. And for his fifth & twentieth parte they did take his horse for it. And as for his challenging of other Ministers, he may be ashamed, for it is well knowne he did never any thinge for the Parliament but as he was constrayned. As for that he saith was on gunpowder treason day, the witnesses did not hear him on that day but do averr & will maynteyn it is his usuall course to speake such words when any moneys or armes are to be raised for the defence of kinge & Parliament. And the other other parte of the article the witnesses so likewise averre it to be true. (Thomas Cooper, Thomas Grymwade, Bridget Cooper, Ambrose Bixby).

VII. He saith he never refused to read any ordinance of Parliament; sure he cannot say that ever he read any for the Parliament, nor yet for the Lord Fairfax (that order that was for contribution), nor contributed any thinge himselfe. And wee averr he refused to read those ordinancs which are named in the 7th Article, and did despise the readinge of them, as is sett forth in the said Article. (Ambrose Bixby, Richard Manning).

VIII. He did not take the vow & covenant, and did what he could to hinder others, tellinge some of his parishioners both in privat & publiq they knew not what they did. Also for that he saith of the bramble & the cedar, it is utterly false and wee averr the contrary; for that of the bramble being above the cedar was spoken in his sermon before the takinge of the covenant, the other words were spoken in the Chancell when the parishioners desired him to take it with them as other godly Ministers did, but wee could not prevayle with him to take it. (Thomas Cooper, Thomas Gibbon, Ambrose Bixby, Thomas Skudgen, Henry Betts).

IX. As for his associatinge, it is answered in the 6th; but he left his parish 3 weekes as is sett forth in the 9th article and wee averr still his usual associates are papists & notorious malignants, and he doth sett such in his place to preach and hath applauded such in his preachinge, as Mr Bolder, Mr Gnash, Mr Hill & others.[1] (Richard Manning, Thomas Cooper, Ambrose Bixby).

X. Wee averr this Article to be true. (Ambrose Bixby, Ralph Hall [now sick of the smallpox]).

XI. He almost confesseth this Article, and he agen affirmeth it to be true. (Edward Cooke).

XII. He did not take the last nationall covenant, according to direction, in his owne parish and did suffer some to sett to their hands that did not heare it all read through his meanes. And he is so unwilling to execute any ordinance the Parliament setts out that either he doth them not all, or elce disorderly. Himselfe did not hold upp his hand in taking it in his owne parish: and so affirm the old article. (*Added in the margin:* Henry Betts testifieth that he sett his hand to it & heard it not read, and Sir Thomas Barker said it was enough to sett hands to it, though they heard it not read.) (Thomas Cooper, James Harlewyne)

XIII. Mr Duncon is desired by our Answerer to name the bookes upon oath, who is ready to give an answer to our answerer. And Ambrose Bixby, being much imployed in working at Mr Keeble's house will averr that he hath been oftentymes called in to hear bookes of newes sett out against the Parliament, but never any for or on behalfe of the Parliament. (Ambrose Bixby).

XIV. That at such tymes as thankes is given for defeats given to the Cavaliers then he contradicts it & saith they have cause to mourne for the bloud of the slayne: and, on the contrary, if he heare the Cavaliers have the victory, as soone after the fight at Braineford, he reioyceth & sayth the winds will fight for god's children. (Thomas Cooper, Thomas Gibbon, Thomas Grymwade, Ambrose Bixby).

XV. That the said Mr Keeble said in his sermon wee must not speake against our Kinge though he be a Pope, or of any religion whatsoever. (James Harlewyne, Thomas Skudgen).

[1] Edmund Boldero, Rector of Westerfield, John Hill, Rector of Thorndon, and Gaven Nash, Rector of St. Matthew's, Ipswich. Hill and Nash had been sequestered in 1643, but Boldero survived until 1647.

XVI. Lastly the said Mr Keeble doth very often sweare by his faith & by his troth, and was reproved by Mr Cole, the Receiver of the 5th & 20th parte for swearinge.[1] (Thomas Cooper, Ambrose Bixby, Daniel Pulford).

XVII. Since our first Articles exhibited, he did by craft gett Mr Devereux, Mr Penn, Mr Springe, Mr Younge[2] to sett their hands to a certificate that Mr Keeble was a laborious preacher etc. To which we do certify that two of them did since confesse that it was neer 20 yeeres since they heard him preach, which was at a lecture at Needham. And we do affirme that he hath seldom or never preached twice on the Lord's day except now of late since he came in trouble. (Bridget Cooper, Thomas Grymwade, Richard Manning).

Witnes the Certificate under Mr Devereux and Mr Springe's hand.

XVIII. Upon oath (Samuel Duncon) testifieth that the bookes he found in Mr Keeble's study were one called 'The King's declaration', and the other he remembreth not. And did then tell Mrs Keeble that there were about a dozen of bookes against the proceedings of Parliament which was a shrewd signe her husband was a malignant, he being at the same time absent from his house and suspected to be at Lestolfe, but confesseth he was at Flixton Hall, at the Lady Tasborowe's, a recusant. (Ambrose Bixby, Thomas Skudgeon, Richard Manninge).

Document 3 (Ms. J. Walker, c. 7, f. 161).

To the Right Honourable the Earle of Manchester, The humble petition of William Keble, Clearke, parson of Ringshall in Suffolk.

Humbly Sheweth that whereas Articles were Exhibited Against your petitioner before the Committee of Parliament for plundred Ministers, whereunto your petitioner Answered & his proofes heard. And uppon heareing your petitioner was thence dismissed, yett with reference to your Lordshipp to doe therein & to examine such further matter concerning the same as to your Lordshipp should seeme meete. After which reference more Articles in nomber butt the same in substance & nature were the 15th day of Aprill last preferred against your petitioner before your Lordshipp's Committee for plundred Ministers sitting at Ipswich in Suffolk, whereunto your petitioner putt in his Answere in writeing & offered his oath to the same & was there ready with 10 or 12 witnesses to prove the truth thereof; but none of his proofes admitted to be heard. After which your Lordshipp beinge enformed of the said Articles & answere, subscribed in these words, "I wish that the informers may reply to this Answere, & produce further Articles if they have any, that my proceedings may bee more satisfyinge to myselfe & others: Manchester." After, uppon the 22th of July last, the Complaynants

---

[1] Jeremy Cole of Stamford, Lincolnshire: the Earl of Manchester's chief agent for the collection of the Fifth and Twentieth Part in Suffolk. For an account of his activities see my thesis, op. cit., pp. 330–1, 462.

[2] Presumably Peter Devereux of Rattlesden, Thomas Young of Stowmarket, Samuel Spring of Creeting All Saints, and John Penne of Old Newton; the latter had been presented to his living by the Keeble family (Norfolk and Norwich Record Office, V.S.C. 2, No. 4: Consignation Book 1636).

did reply unto the said Answere of your petitioner, & did alsoe exhibitt 5 other Articles of the same nature with the former, & alsoe added to some of the former. To which new Articles & additions your petitioner desired to make his Answere & to have a tyme prefixed for his proofe thereof, as by ordinance of Parliament is allowed. But neither Answere nor proofes were admitted nor tyme given, butt one of the committee within three or fower dayes after the exhibiteing of the last aditionall Articles come with the same to your Lordshipp & by some misinformation did obteyne an Eiectment & sequestration against your petitioner in these words, "For superstitious life & an Enemye to the procedings of Parliament.", of both which offences your petitioner doubteth not but to cleere himselfe if admitted his proofes, which is denyed by the Committee, neither can hee obteyne any certificate thereof from them.

Humbly therefore prayeth, for that your petitioner haveing taken the protestation, the association, the nationall League & Covenant, & hath paid his fift & 20th part & all other Parliament Cessis & taxis, that your Lordshipp wilbee gratiously pleased to heere the said Cause att your fitteing opportunity. And the petitioner in the meane tyme to leave the whole tythes to such incombent as the Committee there shall, by your Lordshipp's direction appointe, or the petitioner to procure a curat such as the Committee there shall approve of, & allowe him 20 Markes by the quarter untill your Lordshipp's heareing the same. Only that the petitioner in the meane tyme may have the quiet possession of his house & gleabe, which are about £40 by the yeare, towards the supporte of himselfe, his wife & 5 children.

And your petitioner shall dayly pray, &c.

Chelsey, 16th September 1644.

I desire the Committee have sight of this Petition. And forasmuch as the Petitioner hath taken the Protestation, the Association, the Nationall League & covenant, & hath conformed to all Parliamentary Cesses & taxes, that therefore they permit him to continue the Possession of his house & gleabe till further order from mee. And in the meane tyme the tythes onely to bee imployed towards a Curate, by the Committee allowed or procured. And that they take the Petitioner's answere to the additionall articles & alterations, and that his proofes bee admitted to all upon 14 dayes warninge without oath, & the particular depositions both of plantafe & defendant bee sett downe in writinge & the defendant's Counsell heard (if required) & upon retorne of the proceedinges herein I shall further proceede as Justice shall require.

E. Manchester.

Document 4 (Ms. J. Walker, c. 7, f. 159).

To the Right Honourable the Earle of Manchester, the humble petition of William Keble, clearke, parson of Ringshall in Suffolk.

Sheweth,

That whereas your Lordshipp was pleased uppon your petitioner's

Information of proceedings against him before your Lordshipp's Committee for Plundred Ministers sitinge att Ipswich, as by the petition annexed appeareth, & your Lordshipp did thereunto subscribe That they should take your Petitioner's Answere to the additionall Articles & alterations & that his proofes bee admitted to all uppon 14 dayes warning without oath, & the depositions of Plaintiff & defendant sett downe in writeinge, & uppon retorne thereof your Lordshipp would proceed as Justice should require, as by the petition & subscription appeare. Sithence which tyme your petitioner hath Answered the additionall Articles, wittnesses have bine one both sides exammined & coppyes therof published, and a certificate made to bee sent to your Lordshipp (which if done or not, your petitioner cannot bee informed of). May it therefore please your Lordshipp to cause the same to bee retorned to your Lordshipp by a day certaine, & that your Lordshipp will bee pleased to prefixe a day of hearinge before your Lordshipp att London that your petitioner with his counsell may attend to give satisfaction to your Lordshipp therin, for your petitioner's releife.

And your petitioner shall dayly pray &c.

December 5th 1644.

I doe desire the Committee for Ministers at Ipswich to certify their last proceedings & examination concerning this petition within ten dayes after notice hereof, and upon returne thereof I appoint Mr White, & Mr Smith to heare & end the same, and to certify mee thereof.

E. Manchester.

Document 5 (Ms. J. Walker, c. 7, f. 162).

Whereas uppon the Retorne of the proceedings against Mr Keble, parson of Ringshall, by the Committee sittinge at Ipswich in the County of Suffolk for Scandalous Ministers, I did appointe the same to be heard and Ended by John White Esq., Chayerman of the Committee at Westminster, and Samuell Smith Esq., and am nowe from them Informed that they have accordingly heard the same in the presence of the prosecutor and the said Mr Keble, and that they doe not finde any thinge soe Charged and provede againste him as is in Lawe sufficient Cause for sequestration and Eiectment. And for that he hath ingagede himselfe to mee for the tyme to come to preach, or to procure some able & orthodox divine in his defaulte (he being agede) to preach twice every sonday, and to conforme to all parliamentary proceedings, I doe therefore require all Committees and other officers whatsoever from hence forth quietly to permitte and sufferre him, the said Mr Keeble, to take all the tythes, profitts and benefitts of the said parsonage without molestation or disturbance, untill it shall be made appeare to mee that hee doth not performe his Ingagements aforesaide.

Given under my hand the 24th of Januarye 1644 [*i.e. 1645*]

E. Manchester.

III. The Case of George Carter, Rector of Elmsett and of Whatfield

The nine letters which comprise the third section of this edition, are from the Reverend George Carter to Sir Simonds D'Ewes, M.P. for Sudbury and the diarist of the Long Parliament.

When George Carter, who had held the livings of Whatfield and Elmsett in plurality since 1599, was prosecuted by the parishioners of the latter, he endeavoured to enlist influential assistance, and appealed for help from D'Ewes on the grounds of their kinship. In fact Carter was related to the Cloptons of Liston, a cadet branch of the Cloptons of Kentwell Hall in Long Melford, the heiress of which family had been D'Ewes's first wife.[1] But despite the very distant relationship, D'Ewes, who was conscious of his own parvenu status in the county and consequently inordinately proud of his marriage into one of the most ancient Suffolk families, appears to have welcomed the opportunity to assist "the meanest of . . . [his] . . . first wife's kindred", and became Carter's active patron in the affair.

The history of the case itself is complicated. Carter was first articled against by his Elmsett parishioners in December 1644, the case coming before the Ipswich Committee for Scandalous Ministers for them to report to the Earl of Manchester for final determination. For the next four months Carter endeavoured to secure a favourable hearing from the Earl through the influence of such friends as D'Ewes. But by March 1645 Manchester had resigned from his post as Major-General of the Eastern Association, and it was suggested that those cases which would have been decided by the Earl now devolved upon the Parliamentary Committee for Plundered Ministers at Westminster. Carter favoured the proposed alteration, hoping that his case would now be heard before "gentlemen of worth," not the Ipswich Committee, which he considered both to be wholly biased against him and to consist of his social inferiors; and while still petitioning Manchester, he worked to secure the support of those M.P.s who might be expected to hear the case. In May 1645 the Ipswich Committee were still examining the case on warrants from the Earl, which, according to Carter, they maliciously interpreted in his opponent's favour; but in July the case was taken over by the Westminster Committee.[2] However, the latter, instead of ordering the complete re-trial of the case before themselves which Carter had desired, merely instructed the Ipswich Committee to complete their examinations and to forward the relevant documents to London. Unfortunately there are no letters from Carter for this period, so his feelings about

---

[1] See the pedigrees in Muskett, op. cit., Vol. 1, pp. 143–5.
[2] Add. 15669, f. 119.

this decision are unknown, but he must have been gratified by the sharp rebuke which the Westminster Committee gave the Ipswich Committee in September[1] for not taking Carter's Answer in full, but only "in a Marginall way". The Ipswich Committee were ordered to re-examine the witnesses, and to return full copies of the depositions and answers:[2] this must have been completed by the 15th November, when the hearing at Westminster was postponed until March in view of the approach of winter and the consequent difficulty of travelling for a man of Carter's age.[3] Pressure of business enforced a further adjournment in March,[4] and it was not until the 23rd July 1646 that the Westminster Committee finally decided that Carter should be sequestered from the living of Elmsett.[5]

The reasons by which the Committee came to this decision are not recorded, but it is unlikely that they were swayed by the improbable stories of Carter's lecherous behaviour as they allowed him to keep the living of Whatfield.[6] It is more likely that they saw Carter as a pluralist holding two livings each valued at £100 a year, disenabled by age from giving proper attention to both, and refusing, perhaps incapacitated by his debts, to make any proper provision for the maintenance of a Curate at Elmsett.[7]

The letters are of the greatest interest, and add much to the bare bones of the charges and procedural arrangements recorded in the Committee minute book. They display the accused minister's distress, a compound of righteous indignation at the nature of the charge and fear of the financial consequences for his family should they be pressed home, and they give some account of the tactics employed by both the parties. But perhaps their most valuable function in this edition of the proceedings of the Suffolk Committees for Scandalous Ministers is the insights they give into the 'unofficial' procedures employed by the Ipswich body, and the bitter cameos they contain of that "company of Tradesmen Committees".

---

[1] *Ibid.*, f. 171.

[2] The Westminster Committee addressed their new demands for an examination of witnesses to the 'Committee of Parliament for Suffolk', which would be the Committee sitting at Bury. While it is possible that Carter's protests against the prejudice of the Ipswich Committee had met with some response, the Westminster Committee appear to have confused the two bodies on several occasions (Add. 15669, f. 176), so the point is debatable.

[3] Add. 15669, f. 207v. This reference in the Westminster Minute Book fixes the date of Carter's eighth letter to D'Ewes.

[4] Add 15670, f. 40.

[5] *Ibid.*, f. 165.

[6] It appears from the Whatfield parish register that Carter remained as Incumbent there until his death in 1649. (I am indebted to Mr Norman Scarfe for this information.)

[7] In his ninth letter to D'Ewes, Carter states that he has employed a 'Plundered Minister' to assist him at Elmsett, and that he has agreed to pay him £40 a year. However, in March 1646 the Westminster Committee had to make an order to enforce Carter to pay his assistant, Mr Slany, the promised sum (Add. 15670, f. 40).

I

1644 31st. December. Whatfield. Carter to D'Ewes.

[Harl. 387, f. 27]

Noble knight,

Your happy inclination & disposition to workes of mercy & charity (wherof I have heretofore had good experience) encourage mee in this tyme of my urgent misery to repayre unto your worshipp for shelter in a storme. I prayse God humbly for it, I have all my life-tyme hitherto lived in good esteeme & repute amongst my Parishioners, & was never accompted scandalous any maner of way. Till now of late that one Dubble of my parish of Elmesett, one whom I lately prosecuted for a Bastard begotten & borne in his house, hath secretly by way of revenge stirred up diverse ejusdem farinae[1] of Elmesett, meane Parishoners of mine there, to article against mee before the Committee at Ipswich. Before whom I am to give in mine answere to their scandalous Articles upon Monday next. Mr Francis Bacon & Mr Tirell of Gipping of the Committee (with the other 3, Mr Bloys, Mr Dunkon & Mr Fisher of Ipswich) have used me very lovingly & have found out the malice of that Dubble against mee, & they all will joyne in a favourable & just returne of my case to the Earle of Manchester next weeke. In the meane tyme I thought fitt to addresse these my letters unto your worshipp, humbly desyring you that you would be pleased to deliver my Petition to the right Honourable the Earle of Manchester, (which my sonne Warner, the bearer hereof, shall deliver unto you) eyther this end of the weeke or in the beginning of the next, to prepare his Honour for favour towards me according to the Tenour of my Petition. And wheras I have a Certificate from the chiefest of my 2 small Parishes & from diverse gentlemen & chiefe yeomen of the neighbouring townes neare mee, who under their severall hands have testified of my life & conversation & of my carriage in my Ministeriall function, I shall intreate Mr Bacon & the rest of the Committees to send them up to the Earle next weeke (God willing) when they returne this cause unto his Lordshipp. For truly, Sir Simond, if my Lord should take away one of my Benefices from mee he were as good to take away my life, considering my debts, my deare wife & loving children (lately 11 in number), & mine owne decaying yeares, having already (in the course of nature) one foote in the grave. I doe therfore once agayne most humbly crave your countenance & best assistance in this my deplorable condition, for which your Christian favour you shall ever oblige mee in all bonds of gratitude unto you. Wherupon relying, mine & my poore disconsolate wife hir duety, love & service remembred unto your good worshipp, I humbly take my leave committing you & all yours to the sacred goodnes of our gracious God, always remayning your worshipp's poore kinsman & faythfully affected friend to be commaunded.

[1] Men of the same stamp.

II

1645 4th. March. Whatfield. Carter to D'Ewes.

[Harl. 387, f. 26.]

Noble Sir,

I render most humble & hearty thanks unto your good worshipp for the favour which by your meanes & for your sake I hope I shall receyve from that Honourable Lord, the Earle of Manchester, that I may peaceably enjoy my 2 petite villages during my life. For my better security wherof, (if I might presume so farre of your worthy favour) I would & doe humbly desyre you to procure (as you shall think fitt) a Tickett to that effact under my Lord's hand. And that you would be pleased to deliver this my second Petition unto his Lordshipp which my daughter, the bearer hereof, will present unto you. And least I should suffer any thing eyther in his Lordshipp's judgment, or in your owne opinion, by reason of those malitious Articles which some of my peevish meane Parishoners of Elmesett have most uniustly exhibited against mee, I humbly desyre your worshipp that you would be pleased to read over my answere to every one of those Articles, which answere is of mine owne hand-writing; whereby I doubt not but you shall easily find out mine innocency & their malice. For if I, that have lived 45 yeares in marriage with a good wife as lovingly & comfortably as ever any man did, should now at these yeares & in these tymes of mine owne particular miseries be so vitiously inclined as those base women pretend, it were pitty I should live & I might justly be ashamed once to sett pen to paper, eyther to your worshipp or to any other person of worth. But I hope the Certificates which I sent your worshipp by my Sonne lately will sufficiently vindicate mee from all those vild & scandalous aspertions, both in your worshipp's opinion & in my Lord of Manchester's likewise; in which case I could procure 1000 hands in Suffolk for mine innocent & upright course of life, if neede were. Casting my selfe therfore upon your wonted favour, I humbly take my leave, commending your worshipp & all yours unto the sacred goodnes of our mercyfull God, remembring mine & my deare wife hir most humble service & faythfull affection unto you, always remayning,

your worshipp's assured friend & thankfull kinsman to be commaunded.

III

Undated. Carter to D'Ewes.

[Harl. 387, f. 25.]

Worthy Sir Simonds,

I am bold still to be troublesome unto your worshipp craving the continuance of your favour towards mee. I have herein inclosed sent you a letter from an honest worthy gentleman, the youngest brother of Liston-hall who lived some tyme in my Parish, & therfore is the fitter to testifie of mee. Sir Nathanael Barnardiston[1] came last weeke downe into the countrey, who is

[1] For Barnardiston, see above, p. 50, note 1.

acquainted with my cause by this gentleman, & by his elder Brother, who are neare in bloud to Sir Nathanael, & hee hath promised them his readyenes to joyne with your worshipp in speaking for mee. I was likewise last weeke with old Mr Gurdon,[1] who hath knowen mee these 40 yeares & above, & he hath promised mee to write this day to his sonne Mr John Gurdon[2] for mee to affoord mee his testimony to him. I shall also next weeke (God willing) send up a letter from a neare kinsman of Mr Cage's of Ipswich[3] to Mr Cage with his report of mee; which Mr Cage hath likewise knowen mee these many yeares past. Thus have I endeavoured to strengthen my selfe by your worshipp & these other worthy gentlemen of our countrey, so much the rather because Sir Nathanael told my Cosin John Clopton at Braintree last Thursday that the Earle of Manchester dealt no longer in ministers' causes, which if it be so, then I humbly desyre your worshipp that mine Adversaries (if they doe persist in prosecuting their malicious courses against mee, before the Committee at Westminster) may be compelled to beginne ab initio, & to object & proove against mee what they can. For which, as for all former favours of your worshipp towards mee, I shalbe yett further engaged in the tye of perpetuall thankfullness unto you. For I had rathere a great deale the busynes should be so carryed to be heard before gentlemen of worth then to be slubberd up by a company of Tradesmen Committees here at Ipswich, who have countenanced my adversaries & endeavoured (some of them) to discountenance & vilifie mee. But I leave this to your wisedome, & my selfe to your love, & your worshipp & yours to the gracious goodnes of our mercyfull God, remayning ever your worshipp's poore, allis to be commaunded.

1645 9th. March. Thomas Clopton to D'Ewes. [Harl. 384, f. 141.]

Worshipful Sir,

For all the favoures you have shewed to me at severall times I humbly thanke you & shall acknowledge your noblenes & readynes to doe any curtisy for the meanest of your first wife's kindred, my cosen Carther of Whatfilde who have bin falsely accused of some of his parrish which are knowne to be very base livers & he to be accusd of such crimes as he is knowne to be cleare of & will be justified by all the best of the parish. Sir, if you had not stucke to him & he had bin throwd out of his livinge the man had bin utterly undone, havinge a wife & a great charge of children. He doth acknowlege this favour of yours in his greatest exspresiones & I hope, Sir, you shal never have cause to repent you. This much I can say, that in raginge time of the Bishopes, he was a great frend of many godly ministers & a great meanes to keepe them in thire livinges. Thus with my respectes to you & your noble lady presente, I remaine Your pore kinseman & servant.

---

[1] Brampton Gurdon of Assington (Died 1647: Muskett, *op. cit.*, I, pp. 286–7).

[2] John Gurdon of Great Wenham (1595–1679). M.P. for Ipswich in the Long Parliament.

[3] William Cage of Ipswich and Burstall (1575–1645). Gurdon's fellow-member for Ipswich.

IV

1645 25th. March. Whatfield. Carter to D'Ewes.   [Harl. 387, f. 28.]

Good Sir Simonds,

I humbly desyre your worshipp still to stand by mee to my Lord of
Manchester, otherwise I am utterly undone. One Downes, a poore Taylour
of my Parish of Elmesett, one that is generally defamed for keeping the wife
of one Layt a poore Labourer of that Parish, hath beene lately at London &
brought up the Articles which have beene most uniustly exhibited against
mee, but whether he brought up answere under mine owne hand (to which
I am ready to make oath for the trueth therof) I knowe not. And this
Downes brought up with him one Tillott, a poore labouring-man of another
Parish, a bold rude fellow, to be his spokes-man. And they have so prevayled that I shalbe presently cast out of Elmesett unlesse your worshipp
stand my good friend, which I intreate you, even in the bowels of Christ
Jesus, to doe. For what mine accusers are, both men & women, that mine
answere doth fully sett forth, which I desyre your worshipp to enquire after,
& to intreate the Earle to peruse it. And as for mine estate, I am a prisoner
to the King's Bench upon 4 severall Executions, though (by the favour of
Sir John Lenthall, which I pay well for) I am here to looke to my flock; &
this Parsonage of Elmesett I have wholly designed towards the payment of
my debts, which are at the least £700. And £40 per annum I have reserved
out of Whatfield for the same purpose. Now if Elmesett be taken from mee,
I must perish in the common prison of the King's Bench, to the utter
undoeing of my deare wife & children, which to prevent I humbly intreate
your worshipp's best assistance. And to that end I further desyre your
worshipp to speake with Mr John Gurdon[1] of our countrey, one of the
Burgesses for Ipswich, who (as I understand) is made by these 2 fellowe.
against mee: to whom I would have written, but that I am straighted of times
These 2 fellowes were sent downe by my Lord & Mr Ashe (to which Mr Ashe
& Mr Good I have made friends likewise) to procure the hands of the Committee at Ipswich to the proceedings against mee. God be for mee as the
Principall, and your worthy selfe as the Instrument. In confidence of both
which I humbly take my leave, & rest your good worshipp's ever-obliged.

(P.S.) I desyre to heare by my daughter, the bearer hereof, what your
worshipp doth for mee, humbly thanking you for all your former paynes &
kindnesses. If I must needes lose Elmesett I pray, Sir, moove my Lord that
I may have £20 per annum out of it, which is not above the 5th part, considering that I have served the Cure & payd all payments to the Parliament
ever since last Harvest, which is now above halfe a yeare since. Or otherwise
(if I may hold it) I will allowe £50 per annum to a Minister whom the Parish
shall choose to officiate there.

---

[1] It is ironic that Carter should make such a request. It appears from his Diary of the Long
Parliament that D'Ewes detested Gurdon. Hostility towards Gurdon's radical political views
was sharpened by violent personal antipathy. See, for example, Harl. 163, f. 740v.

V

Undated. Carter to D'Ewes. [Harl. 387, f. 24.]

I understand by my daughter Harris, the bearer hereof, what extraordinary paynes you have under-gone, & what infinite kindnes you have shewed towards mee, in going to the Earle of Manchester for mee to countenance mee in just defence against my malicious adversaries & that you have prevayled with his Lordshipp that I shall hold my livings during my life & that the prosecutor against mee had a repulse at my Lord's hands for pursuing mee so violently without any just cause, & meerely out of malice. For which your worshipp's undeserved favour I, & my deare wife & children shall, whilst wee live, stand infinitely bound in all due thankfullness unto your good worshipp, for had not you thus stood my friend these base, vitious, malicious enemyes of mine would have [*trium*]phed over mee & even trampled upon mee. But I humbly prayse my [*God for*] stirring up so worthy a friend as your good selfe to stand for mee & [*vindi*]cate my credit by keeping mee in my Livings, wherby I shalbe the better [*able*], (through God's blessing) to provide for my deare wife & children, & to pay my [*debts*]. And (by the grace of God) I will endeavour so to carry my selfe in my Ministeriall function, & in the whole course of my conversation, that your worshipp shall never repent you of doing these kindnesses for mee. For the fuller perfecting wherof I humbly desyre Your worshipp once more to repayre to the Earle for mee & to procure a Tickett under his Lordshipp's hand that hee is pleased to suffer mee to enjoy my 2 small Parsonages during my life or (at the least) to require my Parishioners of Elmesett not to trouble themselves or mee in moving any more against mee. By which conclusive act of yours you shall yett further oblige mee & mine unto your worshipp for ever, wherin hoping of your continued favour (therby to stopp the clamours & querelous complaints of my most envyous Parishioners) mine & my wive's most humble service & thankfullness remembred to your good worshipp, with our dayly prayers unto God for his favours & blessings to be reached out to you & yours, I betake you to his sacred goodnes, resting ever your worshipp's assured thankfull friend in all Christian duetyes to be commaunded.

Parts of this letter are damaged; conjectural readings for missing words are enclosed in square brackets.

VI

1645 13th. May. Whatfield. Carter to D'Ewes. [Harl. 387, f. 29.]

Good Sir Simonds,

Give mee leave (I beseech you) once agayne to acquaint you with the partiall & unjust proceedings of the Committee at Ipswich in my unhappy buysyness, which I intend (God willing) to make knowne to my Lord of Manchester also. The Committee men are Mr Bloys, whose Father was a

Mercer of Ipswich; Mr Brandling, a late Mariner there; Mr Fisher, a woollen-draper there; Mr Dunkon, a Tanner there; and Mr Base, the sequestrator of Recusants' & Malignants'-lands, a yeoman's sonne of high Suffolk whose Father left him not £20 per annum to live of. Mr Francis Bacon hath not beene lately among them, nor Mr Thomas Tyrrell of Gipping, neare Stowe-markett. If eyther of these 2 gentlemen had sitt with the Committee I should have had fayrer dealing then I have found at the hands of the other five. And in trueth, it trencheth much upon my Lord of Manchester's honour to appoint such meane men as the first five are to be of the Committee, before whom their betters must be convented. And thus have these men dealt with mee, viz: wheras it pleased my Lord of Manchester to send down an Order to the Committee at Ipswich in favour of mee, & I doe verily beleeve for your worshipp's sake, which order of his consisted of these 2 branches, the first to desyre them to give mee convenient tyme to produce such wittnesses as could impeach the credit of mine accusers, the second to give mee liberty to bring in such men of credit as might testifie what my conversation hath beene formerly. These first five of the Committee graunted a warrant to mine Adversaries to produce such wittnesses as could justifie the credit of mine Accusers. And that 2nd branch of my lord's Order in their warrant to mee they never mentioned, which I have to shew under their hands; for they graunted their warrant to mee onely for bringing in such wittnesses as could infringe the credit of mine accusers, when as they had a fortnight before given a warrant to mine Adversarie's sollicitor for the contrary. And wheras my daughter Groome came in before them to testifie against one of the queanes that had accused mee, Mr Fisher (who is their Actuary) threatned my said Daughter & told hir openly that shee had beene better have gone 40 miles on hir bare feete then to have come there that day to have spoken any thing against that woman. And he told mee openly that I might aswell have brought in my wife as my daughter to have testified in that case. To whom I was so bold as to reply that, by his favour, there was a difference betweene a wife & a daughter in that course of wittnessing. If I might not be too troublesome to your worshipp I would & doe humbly intreate you that you would be pleased to acquaint my Lord of Manchester with these my just grievances, & so to desyre his Lordshipp to affoord mee such reliefe herein, as in his wisedome & justice hee shall think fitt. For which your undeserved favour you shall yett further oblige mee ever to remayne your worshipp's thankfull & constant Orator to be commaunded.

(P.S.) My Lord of Manchester's Order did beare date the 29th of March last. I desyre your worshipp to tell my daughter, the bearer hereof, where my Lord of Manchester lyeth, for I am informed that hee is gone from Covent-garden.

VII

1645 30th. May. Whatfield. Carter to D'Ewes.   [Harl. 387, f. 30.]

Worthy Sir Simonds,

I humbly prayse God for raysing mee up so firme a friend as yourselfe in these my unhappy troubles, & I doe render unto your worshipp most hearty

& humble thankes for your favour continued towards mee therein. It is true I have formerly written unto you that the Committee were my very good friends, which was true so long as Mr Francis Bacon (who hath knowne mee long) & Mr Tyrrell of Gipping neare Stowe-markett, did sitt with the rest of the Committees; but they sitting of late altogether at Bury, I have not found that equall favour which formerly I did. Mr Bloyse (I confesse) is a good ingenuous gentleman, but much overswayed by the rest. Mr Brandling, who is newly putt into the Commission was of late a Mariner till he matcht with a rich widow. Mr Base had not above £20 per annum left him by his father, a yeoman in high-Suffolk, but he hath beene well increased by a rich widow too. Mr Dunkon now useth the trade of a Tanner. And Mr Fisher, who is the stickler among them, is a woolen-draper; one that by the meanes of Mr Calamy & Mr Newcoman, two Divines of the Assembly,[1] who maryed 2 of Mr Fisher's wive's Sisters, is very powerfull with Mr Ashe & Mr Good, my lord of Manchester his Chaplaynes, & therupon is very buysy & peremptory amongst the Committee, he beeing their Scribe. And his Father, who is living, was the sonne of one of the Common Sergeants in Ipswich who carryed the Mace before the Bayliffes there. These are the men that have slighted mee & used mee very discourteously since the 2 gentlemen, Mr Francis Bacon & Mr Tyrrell left sitting with them. And for ought I can perceyve by them they intend not to send up the testimonyes of my wittnesses upon oath, but Mr Fisher cursorily passeth them over with short imperfect notes, as hee doth his shopp-booke at home. And what may I expect from these men that have neyther good bloud nor breeding in them? I doe therfore most humbly intreate the continuance of your worshipp's favour who am thus most unjustly tost up & downe by meane malitious prosecutors, base [born] accusers & partiall hearers of my cause. I doubt not but your worshipp shall reape much honour by standing up in the cause of an aged, innocent Minister. I doe further desyre your worshipp to move my Lord of Manchester to call for all the examinations of my late wittnesses which I produced to impeach the credit of mine accusers & to shew what my conversation hath formerly beene in the judgment of all able & honest men that have knowne mee, which testimonyes (I feare) Mr Fisher will deteyne from my Lord, & suppresse them unlesse they be called for by the Earle. Thus ceasing to be further troublesome unto your good worshipp at this tyme, mine & my deare wife hir most humble service remembred unto you, I take my leave & rest alwayes your worshipp's much-obliged & thankfull friend to be commaunded.

(P.S.) If your worshipp think fitt, I will come up the next Terme & shew myselfe to the Earle; it may please God that he may the rather commiserate mee.

---

[1] Edmund Calamy and Matthew Newcomen, two of the authors of the 'Smectymnuus' pamphlets, and members of the Westminster Assembly of Divines; both they and Peter Fisher married daughters of Robert Snelling, portman of Ipswich. There are articles on both men in D.N.B.

VIII

Undated, unsigned. (Carter to D'Ewes.)   [Harl. 385, f. 176.]

Good Sir Simonds,

I humbly thank your worshipp for all your favour towards mee & in speciall for the late Order which you obteyned from the Committee for hearing my cause the first Tuesday in March, which I hope will yett be putt off till the next weeke after Easter by your good assistance if the Committee be pleased to consider aright of this warrant herein inclosed, which for that purpose I doe send unto you, desyring you first to peruse it carefully & then to shew it to Mr Millington & to the rest of the Committee, to desyre them to take notice of it. It was served upon mee by one John Hayward of Elmesett, one of my malicious prosecutors, a drunken fellow, upon Saturday last about ten of the clock in the forenoone, to appeare at Westminster this Thursday, November 27th. When I first cast mine eye upon it, I found it to be sophisticated in diverse particulars. This Hayward told mee he receyved it from Mr Farrington their Sollicitour, on friday night last. But I doe evidently perceyve that it was a warrant intended to have given mee notice of my last appearing upon the 23rd of the last moneth, at which tyme I appeared without any warrant; but now it is razed & interlined & altered to serve their turne to have unjustly drawen mee up to London this tedious weather. The insarting of (November) in the second line of the title after October by another hand & the adding of (on the 27th day of November next instant) doe apparantly shew the juggling that hath beene used in it.[1] For I send it to your worshipp as I tooke it from Hayward above named & I desyre you to have a care of it & to deliver it to my daughter, the bearer hereof that shee may lay it up carefully for mee. I humbly desyre to be discharged by the Committee considering how fowly & maliciously mine adversaries doe carry themselves against mee in the maner aswell as in the matter of their proceedings against mee. Or, at the least, I humbly desyre your worshipp upon this occasion, to moove the Committee for the deferring of the hearing of my cause till the beginning of April, for the latter end of February is likely to proove as ill a tyme for travayle as now it is. But I committ these thinges unto your wisedome, & your worshipp & all yours to God's sacred goodnes & preservation, ever remayning.

IX

Undated. Carter to D'Ewes.   [Harl. 385, f. 108.]

Worthy Sir,

I desyre your worshipp to moove the Committee for so much further favour for mee, that the hearing of my cause may be putt off till the first

---

[1] Carter's opponents may not have been as malicious as he suggests. The Westminster Committee did, on 8 November, order Carter's appearance on the 27th of that month; but a week later they rescinded this and issued the warrant for him to attend in March (Add. 15669, ff. 198 v., 207 v.).

Tuesday in April; for if they hold mee to the first Tuesday in March then must I come up by waggon in the last weeke of February at which tyme the wayes use to be as deepe & the weather as cold as in any part of the winter. And that would be hard for a man of my yeares. My malicious Adversaries doe triumphum canere ante victoria, & truly, Sir, it were very harsh for mee to be ejected out of Elmsett upon the bare testimonyes of such lewd & inconsiderable persons without oath. The two chiefe prosecutors of mee, Thomas Downs & John Hayward, make just accompt to out mee, & to gett a Sequestration to be graunted to them & so to come into such moenyes as they have layd out in prosecuting this cause against mee, which is (as they say) neare £40.[1] And one of their wives told mee this day that if I would take some course to pay them their charges they would proceede no further against mee; in which point I desyre your worshipp's opinion. For I have of late entertayned a plundered Minister to be my Coadjutour at Elmesett, to whom I have agreed to give £40 per annum free from all Parliament-payments; and hee is a very sufficient Preacher & one that gives the people very good contentment. Thus beeing bold to lay open my state unto your worshipp, humbly craving the continuance of your favour to mee & my deare wife, in these my unjust molestations, I take my leave, remembring both our humble services & best respects to your good worshipp & to your ver-tuous Lady, & so commending you both & all yours unto God's sacred goodnes & preservation. . . . [*the remainder of this letter, upon which D'Ewes has scribbled some sermon notes, is obliterated.*]

---

[1] Downes, but not Hayward, was appointed sequestrator of the living with William Smith, Esq., and John Blois by the Westminster Committee, 23 July, 1646 (Add. 15670, ff. 165, 227.).

IV The Case against Maptid Violet[1],
Curate at Aldeburgh

This case has a double interest. In the first place it provides the only surviving example of an 'Answer' to a charge by a Suffolk minister. Violet's answer includes, besides a refutation of the specific charges against him, a defence of his conduct in general terms, and an attack on the witnesses against him, as motivated by malice and unworthy of credit – apparently a common line of defence for accused ministers.[2]

Secondly, the accusation is against a man who, at least by his own account, was a vigorous supporter of the Parliamentary cause both financially and 'in my doctrine'. Nor was Violet identified with the Laudians: he was dismissed from his curacy at Carleton Rode by the Rector for his refusal to obey Bishop Wren's Injunctions. One of the charges brought against John Lethwaite, the Rector of Rockland Tofts, before the Norfolk Committee of Scandalous Ministers, was that he had refused to allow Violet or another 'godly minister' the use of his pulpit.[3] Nor was the prosecution motivated entirely by distaste for Violet's drunken behaviour, although this alone is stressed in the Articles against him. In the Aldeburgh archives there is a letter from Thomas Nuttall, Rector of Saxmundham, and John Ward, Rector of St Clements, Ipswich, to Manchester's Chaplain, William Good.[4] Their chief concern is with the immediate issue of a sequestration against Richard Topcliffe, the Laudian Vicar of Aldeburgh, and the induction of an acceptable replacement; but in a postscript they write that the messenger is bringing up the Articles against Violet, 'which base Antinomian is like to be intertayned at Hallisworth & teach them libertinisme who need noe spurres. I wish you could procure a warrant which might scare him to his wife in Norfolk'. The two ministers, both Presbyterians,[5] suggest that Violet is an adherent of the Antinomian doctrine, holding that the moral law does not oblige God's elect,[6] and that, presumably, his own immoral behaviour stemmed from these tenets.

---

[1] His singular first name has been read as Maxtid, but on balance the documents indicate Maptid.

[2] See above, p. 43.

[3] Ms. J. Walker, c. 6, ff. 44, 46.

[4] Ipswich and East Suffolk Record Office, EE 1/P6/6.

[5] Both signed the pro-Presbyterian 'Humble petition of the ministers in the counties of Suffolke and Essex.' (1646)

[6] For the beliefs, and their application, of another Antinomian preacher in Suffolk, see A. L. Morton, "Laurence Clarkson", *Transactions of the Suffolk Institute of Archaeology*, Vol. 26, 1955, pp. 177–9.

The final result of the prosecution is uncertain. Violet does not appear to have been appointed to Halesworth, as Nuttall and Ward feared, but as in 1647 he was appointed Curate at St James Place, a Donative of the City of London, and in 1655 Rector of Beechamwell, a living he retained after the Restoration,[1] it would seem improbable that any permanent sequestration was issued against him.

March 29th 1644. Articles to be exhibited against ——— Violett, (*sic*) Curate at Aldeburgh in the Countie of Suffolk.

The information of Ema Ripine widow: The said Violett Riding from Aldeburgh to London in company with the said Ema Ripine & others, and lazing by the way at Chelmesford, at there Inn at night the said Violett after supper being merry, fell to drinking with some that were in the howse and demeaned himself very uncivilly in words & deeds. And the said Ema Ripine being in bed he taketh a glasse of beere in his hand and goeth to her bed side and urged her to drinke. She refusing, he tould her that he had heard that she would drinke tenn men drunke, with other uncivill speeches. The next day morning she tould him of it, he denyed it, and being wittnessed to him yet notwithstanding he denyed and forsware it. This being about the vii of February last past. And for the said Ema Ripine, she is well knowne to be a woman temperat, civill and of good report & cariage. (*The mark of Ema Ripine*).

The information of Mr George Nun of Aldeburgh predictu, woolen draper: The said Violett being in the howse of Mrs Mary Howldine, a Taverne in Aldeburgh aforesaid, the said George Nun being in the howse, the said Violett having been drinking in company . . . . did say in the hearing of the said Mr Nun these words, I can drinke a world of drinke, I think I have a devill in my belly & I thinke he will never out. And did also say, Come lett us syn, for the more we syn the better we shall be accepted. (*Signed George Nun*).

The information of Mrs Mary Howldine, the wife of Mr Thomas Howldine: The said Violett did speake these words in the howse of the said Mrs Howldine, viz: I can drinke a world of drinke I think I have a devill in my belly, I thinke he will never out. And did further say, Tell not me of a benefice, give me a woman's belly. (*Signed Mary Holding*).

The information of Mr Thomas Howlden of Orford in Suffolk gent. . . .: The said Violet being at Orford about two moneths since [*was*] drinking at an alehowse a day and a night. . . . Also the xxixth day of march last, he being againe at Orford one day and a night . . . did say in the hearing of the said Mr Howlding that he had drunke so much that he must goe lay downe. And the said Mr Howlden saith that he was overgone with beere. (*The mark of Thomas Howldine*).

Also the said Violet remayned at Saxmundham drinking in an Taverne from the Thursday untill the satturday, and a mongst other misdemeaners did pursue a maid, drive her into a chamber whether she fled and was

[1] Matthews, pp. 43, 265, 345–6.

rescued by those wittnesses & others. And in there hearing did offer to pawne his Coat for 16d. to pay the reckoning.

The said Violet being at Saxmundham and having a Jugg of beere brought to him by Elizabeth Prettie, he took her and threwe her over a chayer and used her very uncivilly.

These Articles to which the witnesses are annexed were prooved before us this first day of Aprill 1644. Thomas Tirrell, Nathaniel Bacon, William Bloys, Robert Brewster, John Base, Peter Fisher.

(Ipswich and East Suffolk Record Office EE 1/P 6/5/1.)

The Answer of Maptid Violet, Clarke, late of Aldeburgh in the County of Suffolk, to the Information exhibited against him.

To the first Article he sayth that as he is Confident the best of his [*parishioners*] would be sorry to have their Care & Reputation weighed in the balleance of such wittnesses here produced agaynst him, soe he takes it to harte that yf he should have deserved such An Accusation it should not be made good by the Informers themselves that first pretended the same, most of which wittnesses beeinge very well knowne to be of small, or noe reputation, especially this Charge beeinge of such a nature in it selfe as makes me unworthy the name of a man, much lesse a Christian man or to be a Minister in the service of Jesus Christ yf they could be proved against him by men of any quality or Condition. And he hopes this board will be pleased to Conceive better of him who is a minister of god's word. And for cleeringe my selfe in that particuler Charge I doe here freely offer my Oath, & besides there appeares small probability of truth in them – the words in the Article beeinge Charged to be spoken at the same time, for which two wittnesses beeinge produced are not able to manifest the same, they varyinge in their Testimony. And had they byn true had byn as able to have deposed to the latter parte of the charge (viz: Come lett us sinne Etc., and, Tell not mee of a Benefice Etc.,) as to the first. (Which words wer spoken uppon this Occasion: I beeinge sent for to the place in the Article mentioned by the Baylife of the towne, and havinge drunke A Cupp of beere, the said examinate George Nunn Callinge for more I said, What, dost thou thinke I have A devill in my Belly that I should drinke soe much beere.) Allso I trust that this Board will consider that uppon the varryinge of their Testimonyes there is uppon the matter but one single witnesse agaynst mee.

To the second he sayth it is truth that at the time Alledged in the said Article he was at Oreford, but sayth he stayd there but a quarter of An hower, havinge Occasion of businesse elsewhere, and that he retorned to Orford about three of the Clock in the Afternoone Intendinge to goe to Aldeborough, but the winde and tide beeinge both contrary he was inforced to stay all night. But that I was drinkinge as this Article mentioned, I utterly deny & offer my Oath for the proofe of the same, and likewise the Oathes of those that were there with mee (as Jeremy Cob, Richard Boone & others) yf this board shall be pleased to admitt of the same, who can testifie of my demeanure at that time, for beeinge weary and hungery wee presently called for our suppers, and after supper wee went together to prayers & soe to our bedes aboute eight or nine of the clock that night, & in the morninge, like-wise after duty, wee departed aboute sunn risinge & retorned to Aldeburgh from whence wee came. And to the 29th of March in the article mentioned, it is true that havinge speciall Businesse with Mr Lane, he went thether aboute tenn of the Clock in the morninge & stayed till after dynner & there [*was*] noebody there but him selfe & the famely till this Houldinge came there, who desiringe mee to drinke with him, I refused & sayd, Noe, I have dranke enough already. And for the truth of this I likewise offer my Oath, I humbly Conceivinge that this board will thinke that these words are soe farr from provinge mee in any manner disguised that they are rather a cleere profe to the Contrary. And as for the latter Clause which seemes to be justified by Powes, I conceive it to be an Individuum vagum,[1] for he sayth not that he hath seene mee, hee nor the other examinate Houlding, neither have they layd any particular . . . to which I may give a further Answer.

To the third Article and first parte thereof he sayth that he never lay in Saxmondham but once in all his life, & that was in Winter last & uppon this occasion: he goinge to the Lecture (as he constantly did yf he were at whome) on foote, which is five myles from Aldeburgh, where dyninge with the Ministers, it beeing very late, he stayed there the time mentioned in the Article, in the Company of Mr Sollyes (a divine well knowne in these partes both for his life & conversation & allsoe uprightnesse to the Parliament). But that he remayned drinkinge as in the Article is mentioned I utterly deny, and offer my Oath for the Testamony of the same, as allso the Oath of the said Mr Sollyes yf it may be accepted. Likewise to the residue of the Article: toachinge the pursuite & rescue of any mayde or uncivell usage of any woman there, I utterly denye & offer my Oath for the clearinge of my selfe, humbly desiringe this board or the Judge of this Cause that they would be pleased to take into their Concideration in this time of distractions how easy a thinge it is for men aboundinge with mallice to finde wittnesses to accuse men of our profession to accomplish their owne endes, hoping that they will not condemne me uppon the said Scandalouse Articles, there beeinge but one single Testimony set to every severall Article alledged agaynst me, I having allwayes byn forward in the service of the Parliament, both in my owne particular, as in my doctrine. In which particuler I shall be bould to Chalenge any one that shall be able to accuse me in the least. And for my life and conversation & doctrine, had it byn such as in the said Articles is alledged it would have byn manifest to this board by men of the same towne amonge whom I have had any Conversation since my cominge thether, who could never have done it, for when I offered my poore Mite to the ayde of Sir Thomas Fayerfax, it beeinge demanded who I was, it was answered by Mr Baly Cheny & Mr Baly Blowers in these words, This is our honest Curate, to which [*they*] added then & many times since that the towne of Aldeburgh was happy in having two such able & honest Ministers as it then had, & have boasted of mee to strandgers 20 times: this can Sir

[1] Literally, 'A wandering atom'.

William Constable[1] & Colonell Allen imparte, & many others which I could produce, sufficiently and truely witnesse. And I hope the seeinge of a man in an Alehouse . . . or Taverne in an other towne, beeinge then at a lecture or haveinge other Businesse will not be any convinsing evidence to prove him a drunkard or a frequenter of Alehouses, which if it should, it would be an imputation laid uppon not onely the best men but the Ablest & most faythfull Ministers in this Kingdome. All which I humbly submitt to the Judgment of this Board.

Aetas, conditio, sexus, discretio, fama, Fortuna, atque fides in testibus ista requiras.[2]

(signed Maptid Violet)

Aprill 15 1644. The defence of Mr Violett was exhibited unto us, Nathaniel Bacon, Nathaniel Bacon, William Bloys, Robert Duncon, Francis Brewster, Peter Fisher.

(Ipswich and East Suffolk Record Office EE 1/P 6/5/2.)

---

[1] Sir William Constable, M.P. for Knaresborough in the Long Parliament and one of the Parliamentary commanders in Yorkshire, was empowered by the Commons on the 20th July 1643, to raise contributions and volunteers in Norfolk and Suffolk to assist Lord Fairfax in the north (C.J., III, p. 175). Aldeburgh raised a voluntary gift of £99 on this occasion. (Ipswich and East Suffolk Record Office, EE1/01/1, f. 88.)

[2] The age, condition, sex, reputation, standing, fortune and credibility of witnesses must be examined.

Index of Witnesses

With the name of each witness is given the parish against whose incumbent
the witness gave evidence.

Report of the Council for 1967/68

At the 30th September, 1968, membership stood at 400 including 3 Honorary and 5 Life members, a net increase of 3 on the previous year. It was with the greatest regret that the Council learned of the death of the Earl of Iveagh, K.G., C.B., C.M.G., F.R.S., whose ready and generous support at the time of the inauguration helped to ensure the foundation of the Society.

Sales of volumes to non-members continued to rise and totalled 765 as against 710 in the previous year, as follows (the previous year's totals are given in brackets):

Volume I	7 (18)	Volume VII	14 (29)
Volume II	6 (8)	Volume VIII	66 (178)
Volume III	11 (28)	Volume IX	66 (17)
Volume IV	44 (64)	Volume X	93 (182)
Volume V	9 (15)	Volume XI	139 (84)
Volume VI	59 (87)	Volume XII	141 –

Great Tooley of Ipswich   10 (14)

The continued increase in membership, albeit small, and in casual sales, is particularly gratifying since no publicity was sent out during the year. The result is due in the main to the success of our publications, and not least to good reviews.

Volume VI of Mr. Beckett's edition of John Constable's Correspondence, *The Fishers*, appeared during the year leaving only the painter's lectures and lecture notes to be published in a final volume to be entitled *The Discourses*. The publication of this volume is to be financed out of the sales of the other volumes financed by the Mellon Foundation for British Art. If sales continue at their present level it should not be long delayed. A final prospectus advertising the series will be issued when a firm date for the publication of *The Discourses* has been fixed.

Volume XIII[1], Mr. Derek Charman's edition of the South Elmham manuscripts, was also due to appear during the year, but publication will not take place until 1969 as the work of transcription has been delayed.

Work on the Suffolk Bibliography continues steadily under the Chairmanship of Mr. J. Campbell in Oxford, and a further 2,400 slips for books in Suffolk libraries have been completed by Mr. A. V. Steward who joined the Committee recently.

The accounts still reflect a healthy position. The assets in the main account increased slightly over the year from £1,442 to £1,522 as was to be expected as no publication costs were incurred. However, of the £800 owing to the Mellon Account, £544 17s. 0d. was repaid and the balance of £255 3s. 0d. was utilised in purchasing binding cloth. Both subscriptions and income from sale of volumes were fairly steady.

The Mellon Account also shows a very satisfactory position; sales of volumes were up from £463 to £557 and there was an increase in assets from £307 to £727. This is especially commendable as two volumes, Constable V and VI, were published during the year thanks in the main to the balance of the grant of £7,000 from the Mellon Foundation.

The following Council members are due to retire at the Annual General Meeting in accordance with Rule 7, but are eligible for re-election:

J. Campbell, M.A.	Mrs. M. J. Rowe, B.A.
D. Dymond, B.A.	M. P. Statham, M.A.
A. V. Steward, F.L.A.	

(signed)   L. DOW
Chairman

[1] It is hoped that Mr. Charman's volume will now appear as No. XV.

SUFFOLK RECORDS SOCIETY

Statement of Income and Expenditure for the year ended 30th September, 1968

1966/67	INCOME	£ s. d.	£ s. d.
2,205	Balance Brought Forward		1,442 2 8
500	Grants British Academy Constable IV		
511	Subscriptions	497 17 11	
19	Arrears	3 0 0	
44	Advance	31 0 0	531 17 11
827	Sale of Volumes	941 4 4	
463	Less transferred		
364	to Mellon a/c £559 12 6	567 10 3	
	to Tooley a/c £7 17 9		
68	Tax Refund	88 17 7	
48	Dividends on Investments	48 10 6	
44	Interest on Deposit Account	17 16 2	
492	Refund from Paul Mellon Account		
4,295			£2,502 18 11

1966/67	EXPENDITURE	£ s. d.	£ s. d.
23	Annual General Meeting		20 10 2
1	Stamping Covenants		17 3
202	Petty Cash and Postages		88 18 9
44	Stationery		18 10
5	Storage Charges		4 10 8
1	Type Rent Constable III		
	Publication Costs		
1,334	Constable III – Leslie		
1,145	Webb – Poor Relief in Elizabethan Ipswich		
98	Binding Dictionary of Suffolk Arms		255 3 0
	Purchasing Binding Cloth		
	Transfers to Mellon Account		
	Part of £800 owing, Balance utilised in		
	purchasing Binding Cloth £1,400 0 0	544 17 0	
	Balance of Grants		
	Less expenditure on		
	Constable III £1,335 0 0	65 0 0	
1,442	Balance Carried Forward		609 17 0
			1,522 3 3
4,295			£2,502 18 11

ASSETS AT 30TH SEPTEMBER, 1968

	£ s. d.	£ s. d.
Cash at Bank – Current Account	370 12 5	
Deposit Account	75 19 9	446 12 2
Cash in Hand		25 11 1
Investments at Cost		
£312 16 3 Jamaica 6%	300 0 0	
£700 5% National Development Bonds	700 0 0	
£50 5% National Defence Bonds	50 0 0	1,050 0 0
		£1,522 3 3

I have examined the above Income and Expenditure Account; Paul Mellon Account; Tooley Account and Records Account, together with the books and vouchers relating thereto. I have confirmed the balance at the Bank and verified the investments. In my opinion the accounts and statements of assets are correct according to the books and vouchers submitted.

F. WROE
Hon. Auditor

4th February, 1969

SUFFOLK RECORDS SOCIETY

PAUL MELLON ACCOUNT

Statement of Income and Expenditure for the year ended 30th September, 1968

Income

1966/67	INCOME	£ s. d.	£ s. d.
	Balance Carried Forward		306 14 9
	Grant – Paul Mellon Foundation		
3,467	Constable III & IV	1,028 0 0	
	V		
	VI	2,505 0 0	3,533 0 0
	Sale of Volumes VIII	97 5 0	
246	X	122 7 6	
185	XI	208 12 6	
32	XII	131 7 6	
—			
463	*Less* refund . £2 15 3	557 17 3	
		2 3 0	
8	Deposit Interest		
	Transfers from Main Account		
	Balance of Grants –		
	Pilgrim Trust 900		
	British Academy 500		
		1,400 0 0	
	Less expenditure on Constable III	1,335 0 0	
		65 0 0	
	Part of £800 owing by Main account	544 17 0	609 17 0
			£5,008 12 0
3,938			

Expenditure

1966/67	EXPENDITURE	£ s. d.	£ s. d.
492	Charges Constable III and IV Publication		4,117 2 11
3,091	Constable IV	1,930 0 0	8 8 0
	V		
	VI	2,187 2 11	
8	Type Rent on standing Type		
	Typing Copy of Index		
1	Constable V		
	Indexing Constable VI		26 5 0
39	Postages Volume XI		
	Postages Constable VI		22 8 10
	C. Glasgow Honorarium Constable V		25 0 0
	E.S.C.C. Microfilming Constable II		6 10 0
	H.M.S.O. 50 Copies Constable I plus postage		75 11 6
307	Balance Carried Down		727 5 9
3,938			£5,008 12 0

Assets at 30th September, 1968

	£ s. d.	£ s. d.
Cash at Bank – Current Account	167 5 10	
Deposit Account	559 19 11	
		£727 5 9

127

TOOLEY ACCOUNT

Year ended 30th September, 1968

1966/67	INCOME		£	s.	d.	1966/67	EXPENDITURE		£	s.	d.
60	Balance Brought Forward	..	40	6	8	32	W. S. Cowell Ltd.	..	30	0	0
12	Sales	..	18	15	6	40	Balance Carried Forward	..	29	2	2
72			£59	2	2	72			£59	2	2

RECORDS ACCOUNT

Year ended 30th September, 1968

1966/67			£	s.	d.	1966/67			£	s.	d.
240	Balance Brought Forward	..	31	19	10	2	British Records Association	..	2	10	0
11	East Suffolk County Council	..	100	0	0	223	E. M. Dance	..			
10	Donation	..	10	0	0	32	Balance Carried Forward	..	140	9	5
6	Interest on Deposit Account	..		19	7						
257			£142	19	5	257			£142	19	5

		£	s.	d.
Current Account	..	119	10	6
Deposit Account	..	20	18	11
		£140	9	5